MEDICARE BLUEPRINT™

MEDICARE BLUEPRINT™

A JUST-THE-FACTS APPROACH TO
DESIGNING YOUR MEDICARE BENEFITS

Thanks f-

JASON MACKEY & TIM HANBURY

Published by Advantage, Charleston, South Carolina.
Member of Advantage Media Group.

ADVANTAGE is a registered trademark, and the Advantage colophon is a trademark of Advantage Media Group, Inc.

Printed in the United States of America.

ISBN: 978-1-59932-810-2
LCCN: 2017931708

Cover design by Katie Biondo.
Editing by Ellyn Sanna and Advantage Media Group.

This publication is designed to provide accurate and authoritative information in regard to the subject matter covered. It is sold with the understanding that the publisher is not engaged in rendering legal, accounting, or other professional services. If legal advice or other expert assistance is required, the services of a competent professional person should be sought.

Advantage Media Group is proud to be a part of the Tree Neutral® program. Tree Neutral offsets the number of trees consumed in the production and printing of this book by taking proactive steps such as planting trees in direct proportion to the number of trees used to print books. To learn more about Tree Neutral, please visit **www.treeneutral.com.**

Advantage Media Group is a publisher of business, self-improvement, and professional development books. We help entrepreneurs, business leaders, and professionals share their Stories, Passion, and Knowledge to help others Learn & Grow. Do you have a manuscript or book idea that you would like us to consider for publishing? Please visit **advantagefamily.com** or call **1.866.775.1696.**

To my dad, you worked so hard, for so many years to provide for your family and never complained. You led by example and are part of the generation that made this such a great country.

To Allison, thank you for your unwavering support in this and in all the things I do. I love your quiet strength and your beautiful smile. You're a great mom and I am so blessed to have you in my life.

To my son Alex, you are the "why" in the "what" I do. Sixteen can be a challenging age, but I so enjoy your enthusiasm, your silly humor, and your big heart. In you I see the beginnings of a truly good man in the making. You make your mom and me proud.

Lastly, to my mom who was always there for me and who helped make me the man I am today. I miss you!

—Tim

To my father, Dalton, you have been an amazing mentor and business partner. Your entrepreneurial spirit, integrity, and passion for helping people have been an invaluable guide in my personal and professional life.

To my mother, you have been a great support throughout my life, and I cannot thank you enough.

To my son, Jackson, I will never be able to thank God enough for blessing me with you. You are my motivation to be a better person and work hard every day. Your smile, wit, and laughs are just what I need to keep me going. I am so proud of you, and I want you to know that your hard work and amazing personality will take you as high as you want. I love you more than . . . well, you will know what I mean when you give me some grandchildren.

—Jason

CONTENTS

See our special offer for our readers on page 129.

ABOUT THE AUTHORS

Tim Hanbury is a Registered Health Underwriter (RHU) with more than thirty years of experience in the health insurance business. He was a sales manager for BlueCross BlueShield of South Carolina and a VP of sales for Cigna Healthcare. His expertise includes individual health, group health, and Medicare insurance. He has been an independent insurance agent since 2001 and has helped thousands of individuals navigate the insurance marketplace, specializing in helping individuals with their choices for Medicare coverage. "I especially enjoy helping people with Medicare," Tim says, "as it's one of the few times you can give people what they want—nearly 100 percent coverage at a cost they can afford. It's very satisfying helping people understand their options and getting them the right coverage at the time of their lives when they will need it most."

Jason S. Mackey is a United States Air Force veteran who earned a top-secret security clearance while working on the B-2 Spirit stealth bomber. In 1998, after completing his service, he returned to Charleston, SC, to join his family's insurance agency. They have been an independent insurance agency since

1989, which allows them to build the best solutions for their clients. Upon his father's retirement in 2014, Jason became president of the company. Jason has always had a passion for having a vast knowledge of the Medicare program and guiding people through it. "I really enjoy helping people through the Medicare maze and simplifying the process," Jason says. "I get a lot of satisfaction seeing the relief a person has after designing their plan. The best part is that we can do this at no cost to the client."

FOREWORD

I am pleased to contribute briefly to *Medicare Blueprint* by Jason Mackey and Tim Hanbury. Jason has been a friend and trusted advisor on insurance matters for over ten years.

Since I have been a practicing physician for over thirty years and a Medicare recipient for seven, I feel uniquely qualified to recommend this book to seniors and those participating in the Medicare arena including some medical offices.

This book is written in an inclusive and comprehensive format that is easily understood. Supporting charts and examples guide one through the often-complex Medicare maze. It also explains why using an experienced agent can make it an easier task while often saving you time and money.

I think you will find *Medicare Blueprint* can bring clarity to those entering this "chapter" of their Medicare lives. You can visit their website at MedicareBlueprint.com to register for your complimentary copy.

Respectfully,
William J. Fogle III, MD
Physicians Eyecare Network, Founder

INTRODUCTION

A gentleman named Thomas was recently referred to us. Thomas was already retired and about to turn sixty-five. He had a retiree medical plan through his former employer, and he thought it was expensive. He had spoken with several advisors over the phone who told him, "Sign up for Medicare Part B when you turn sixty-five, and just keep your employer's retiree plan" and promptly hung up. We suspect that these advisors didn't think they could make a sale, so they didn't think Thomas was worth their time.

We didn't feel that way. We took the time to compare a Medicare Supplement Plan to Thomas's employer's retiree plan in terms of premiums, deductibles, copays, and annual out-of-pocket costs. We were able to determine that the Medicare Supplement Plan premium and out-of-pocket were significantly lower. We then helped him enroll in Medicare Part B and a Medicare Supplement Plan. We gave him a blueprint he could follow to construct the insurance coverage for his needs.

As Thomas discovered, Medicare is complex and confusing. We're sorry; we wish it weren't, but it is. That's why we have written this book: to give more people like Thomas the blueprint they need to build a future with the coverage they deserve (and have paid for all these years).

If you're starting to think about Medicare, or if you're already feeling frustrated and confused by the process of enrolling, you *could* order or download a copy of "Medicare and You" from Medicare.gov. (When you go to the website, you'll see "Publications" at the bottom of the page.) This 150-plus-page document will provide you with the information you need to know—but it's not an easy read. And do you really have time in your busy life to read the entire thing and put it all together in your mind? In our experience, what people really want is someone who can walk them through the process and explain what they are getting.

Creating your Medicare blueprint is a little like putting together a jigsaw puzzle. It's made of a bunch of pieces that really do fit together—we promise—but at first glance, it can seem like an overwhelming and nearly impossible task. Once you have the corners and sides in place, though, you can start to fill in the middle, and then, all of a sudden, you see the picture. Like a jigsaw puzzle, drawing up your Medicare blueprint isn't really that hard; it just takes some time. We can make sure you have all the individual pieces and haven't missed any. Then it just takes a little longer to see the whole picture take shape.

In this book, we are first going to focus on the "edges and corners" of Medicare—what you need to do to get signed up for or to opt out of certain parts of Medicare at age sixty-five and beyond. We will concentrate on the two most common scenarios that seniors will encounter, which are called the Initial Enrollment Period (IEP) and a Special Enrollment Period (SEP). The IEP is when you are turning sixty-five, and an SEP usually occurs when you continue working and are covered under your employer's (or your spouse's employer's) health insurance plan.

There are different considerations for each scenario, and your needs depend on your unique situation. This is not a one-size-fits-all type of thing. Our goal for this book is for you to quickly learn the Medicare facts you need to make the best choice for your coverage while steering you away from extraneous and confusing information.

We also recommend that you use a local agent to help you in this process. Believe it or not, most Medicare plans are sold by call centers. You see some of these on TV, with the thirty-second to thirty-minute commercials highlighting the benefits of a single company's plan. Many are available online by searching "Medicare." Please understand, we are not saying that these people won't do a good job in helping you pick a plan. They certainly might. However, call center employees are never going to call you back to see how things are going, and they are never going to be there to answer questions or handle claims issues. If you call them back, it's unlikely that you'd be able to talk with the same person you talked to the first time. None of that is in their job description; they sell Medicare insurance policies, and that's it.

However, a local agent will be there to help you today and in the future. If you get a good one, he or she will follow up with you and keep you aware of changes to Medicare. If you have a claims issue or just a question about all the paperwork, you can call and get help. Most important, the cost of this personalized service is included in the cost of any plan you choose. You don't pay any more for a local agent's services than if you purchased the plan directly from the insurance company or a call center. Doesn't it make sense to buy from someone you know—who can sit with you, face-to-face—than from some anonymous voice on the phone?

As for us, we have decades of experience working with seniors and with Medicare—and we love our work! There is no other time in your life when health insurance is more important than when you are sixty-five or over. Now let's get started on your blueprint for the future!

MEDICARE 101

Understanding Its History and Purpose

In 1961, when Doris was diagnosed with a serious level of adult-onset diabetes, she knew she was in trouble. The sixty-seven-year-old widow had no health insurance. On her limited income, she had no idea how she was going to pay for insulin, needles, and all the ongoing health care she would require.

When Doris's husband was still alive, his work had provided health insurance for both of them, but Don had died of a heart attack when he was only sixty-one. After Don's death, Doris had tried to buy health insurance for herself, but she could not afford the premiums because of her age. Over the past few years, she had lain awake some nights, worrying about what she would do if she were to have an accident or become seriously ill—but Doris seldom even got sick with a cold, so she tried to put her concerns out of her mind. She prayed that she would be lucky enough to keep her good health for many years to come.

But with the diabetes diagnosis, Doris's good luck had run out, and there was no solution to her problems in sight. She hated to be a burden on her adult children, but she didn't know what else she could do.

Just a few years later, though, the US government added amendments to Social Security legislation and created Medicare. President Lyndon B. Johnson signed it into law in 1965. By the following year, Doris was able to receive publically funded health coverage.

THE EARLY DAYS OF MEDICARE

As far back as the days of President Teddy Roosevelt, the US government had been aware that seniors faced a health crisis. In 1912, a national health plan was part of Roosevelt's platform when he ran for president, but it didn't gain steam until more than thirty years later, when President Harry S. Truman called for the creation of a national health insurance fund, open to all Americans. The plan Truman envisioned would have paid for such typical expenses as doctor visits, hospital visits, laboratory services, dental care, and nursing services. Although Truman fought to get a bill passed during his presidency, he failed, and it was another twenty years before Medicare became a reality. The very first Medicare card was issued to former president Truman.

During Medicare's first year, nineteen million individuals signed up for it. Today, Medicare continues to provide health care to people like Doris. By 2015, Medicare provided health insurance for over forty-six million people age sixty-five and older as well as for nine million younger people.[1]

WHAT EXACTLY *IS* MEDICARE?

Everyone knows the word "Medicare," but many people are a little foggy as to what exactly it means. The shortest definition is this: it's a federal system of health insurance for people over sixty-five years of age and for certain younger people with disabilities. But let's break it down a little bit further.

The federal government manages the Medicare program, but it partners with hundreds of private insurance companies to do so. Medicare covers about half of the health care charges for those enrolled. The other half has to come from other sources: supplemental insurance, separate insurance, or out-of-pocket. We'll talk about all of these later on in this book.

WHY IS MEDICARE NEEDED?

In the early 1960s, more than half of all Americans over sixty-five were in the same boat as Doris: they lacked private health insurance. Private insurance companies were reluctant to insure

---

1   "2016 Annual Report of the Boards of Trustees of the Federal Hospital Insurance and Federal Supplementary Medical Insurance Trust Funds," Centers for Medicare & Medicaid Services (June 22, 2016): 7. https://www.cms.gov/Research-Statistics-Data-and-Systems/Statistics-Trends-and-Reports/ReportsTrustFunds/downloads/tr2016.pdf.

older people, because those people tended to use much more medical care than younger ones. Due to the increased risk, insurance premiums for older people needed to be high, but the average elderly person was retired and unable to pay such high premiums.

The solution was government-administered health insurance that's funded in the same way as Social Security. By paying in contributions while working—when people can afford to make payments—the program provided protection without further payments during retirement. To put this simply: the money that pays for this insurance comes mostly from payroll taxes. As with any kind of insurance, some people will pay in more than they receive back, and others will get back more than they paid in. That's how all insurance—both public and private—works. But ultimately, your hard work paid for your Medicare insurance. You've earned it!

P L E A S E

☐ Medicare is a form of health insurance that's managed by the federal government.

☐ During your working life, portions of your payroll taxes are the "premiums" that pay for your future Medicare coverage.

WHAT DOES THAT MEAN?

Understanding Medicare Terminology

Eric is sixty-four years old, and he's thinking about retiring in the next year or two. When he leaves his job, he'll no longer have health insurance. He saw an advertisement on television for a number he could call to get more information about Medicare, so that's what he did. Now he's on the phone, trying to take notes as he listens to the person on the other end of the line run through what he'll need to do in order to apply.

"First," she says, "you need to decide if you want Original Medicare or a Medicare Advantage Plan, like an HMO or PPO. Then we'll need to decide if you want prescription drug coverage—that's Part D. Do you know if you will also want supplemental coverage?"

Eric doesn't know what to say. He doesn't understand the question. "Could you explain a bit more?" he asks. "I don't understand what those terms mean."

"Well," the voice in his ears says, speaking very slowly now. "Like I said, you can choose Original Medicare or a Medicare Advantage Plan. Okay?" It doesn't matter how slowly the woman speaks, though. Eric still can't understand what she's talking about. "If you want Part D," the woman continues, "that's prescription drug coverage, okay?"

"Okay," Eric says, glad to hear something that makes sense.

"If you opt for Part D, you're going to need to look over the formulary."

Now Eric is lost again. What's a "formulary"? As the woman keeps talking, Eric tries to follow along as best he can, jotting down all the unfamiliar terms and acronyms. He figures that when he gets off the phone, he can look up everything and try to make sense of it all. Pretty soon, though, his eyes are glazing over, and he's totally lost. There are just too many sets of letters sprinkled among the woman's words—IEP, AEP, PFFS, PPO— for Eric to keep up with.

MEDICARE TERMINOLOGY

Eric's not the only one who gets confused when he tries to understand the Medicare process. Pretty much all the people we work with, when they start talking and reading about Medicare, find that a lot of the terms can be confusing and overwhelming.

To start with, let's define the most basic Medicare terms: Part A, Part B, Part C, and Part D:

Part A covers the nursing care and other services you receive if you have to be in a hospital, nursing home, or rehab center. You don't pay a premium for Medicare Part A, because it was paid for by all the years of deductions from your paychecks. At age sixty-five, if you have worked at least forty work credits (equivalent to at least ten total years of working while paying into Medicare and Social Security), you are entitled to Medicare Part A at no cost to you. There are several other ways to qualify for Part A; these depend on various factors, including your spouse's work credits. You can also purchase Part A coverage if you do not qualify for it.

Part B covers medical services you receive as an out-patient—things like shots, lab tests, mental health care, doctor visits, and some medical equipment and supplies (such as walkers or supplies for diabetics). Part B does have a premium you must pay; how much you pay will depend on your income.

Part C is an alternative to "Original Medicare," which is what we just described in Parts A and B. Part

C includes a range of health plans that are administered by private insurance companies but paid for (in part) by Medicare. This is also known as "Medicare Advantage," and by law, such plans must cover all the same services that would normally be covered by Parts A and B (but may also offer additional benefits). Your out-of-pocket costs for Part C may be quite different, however, from what they would be with Original Medicare.

Part D is insurance for outpatient prescription drugs. That sounds simple, but it's a complicated process we discuss further in chapter 7. Most Part C plans will also include Part D.

FOUR PARTS OF MEDICARE

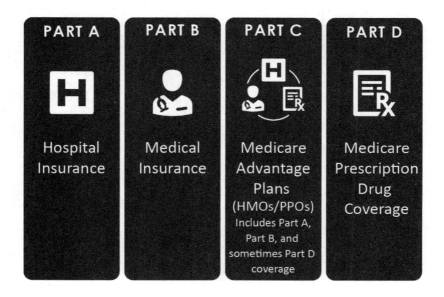

PART A	PART B	PART C	PART D
Hospital Insurance	Medical Insurance	Medicare Advantage Plans (HMOs/PPOs) Includes Part A, Part B, and sometimes Part D coverage	Medicare Prescription Drug Coverage

There are other Medicare plans that also use letters, but these are the four "parts" you'll encounter most often when you start gathering information about Medicare.

As Eric discovered, there are a lot more terms beyond the alphabet soup that refer to various Medicare plans. We'll be using many of these terms in this book, so we thought we'd offer a glossary at the beginning of the book instead of at the end.

Read it over to familiarize yourself with the words and abbreviations, but don't feel as though we expect you to memorize them all now. We'll make things as clear as possible as we go along. In case you get confused, though, you can always flip back to this section. You can also refer to this glossary whenever you're reading or talking to someone about Medicare and run into something you don't quite understand. And if you still have questions, we'd be happy to talk with you on the phone.

MEDICARE GLOSSARY

Advance Beneficiary Notice (ABN): The document (given by a doctor or health-care provider to a patient receiving health-care benefits through Medicare) stating that a procedure or service may not be covered under Medicare. This notice must be given before the procedure or service is provided. If a patient does not receive an ABN and Medicare does not cover their procedure or service, the patient may not have to pay for it. If the patient does receive an ABN and signs it, and Medicare does not cover the procedure or service, the patient may have to pay for it. ABNs are applicable to beneficiaries enrolled in Original Medicare (Parts A and B) but not beneficiaries enrolled in Medicare managed care plans or private fee-for-service plans.

Annual Election Period (AEP): The period of time, from October 15 through December 7, during which people who are Medicare-eligible can enroll in, disenroll from, or change to the Medicare Advantage or Medicare prescription drug plan of their choice for the following year. This does not apply to Medicare Supplement (Medigap) policies.

Annual Notice of Change: In September of each year, Part D and Medicare Advantage Plans must send a letter to their enrollees specifying changes in benefits and cost that will affect them the following year.

appeal: A request submitted by a Medicare beneficiary for reevaluation of a decision made by Medicare or a Medicare plan regarding payment or patient eligibility for a health-care service, drug prescription, or medical product or a change in the amount that must be paid by the beneficiary for a service, product, or procedure.

assignment: The agreement a participating doctor, supplier, or health-care provider makes to accept payment from Medicare for the Medicare-approved amount for a service or procedure, ensuring that beneficiaries pay only the deductible and coinsurance amounts.

beneficiary: A person whose health-care benefits are provided through Medicare or Medicaid.

benefit period: The period of time during which Medicare will pay for hospital and nursing services. A benefit period begins the day a beneficiary enters the hospital and ends after the beneficiary has not received any hospital or nursing care for sixty full days in a row. There is no limit on the number of benefit periods a beneficiary may have in his or her life, but the beneficiary must pay a new deductible for each benefit period.

coinsurance: The percentage of costs of covered medical services or prescriptions that you pay out-of-pocket after already having paid the plan's deductible (i.e., 80/20, where Medicare pays 80 percent of costs and you pay 20 percent).

copayment: The fixed amount you pay for a covered health-care service when you receive medical services or have a prescription filled.

cost sharing: The total amount of money a beneficiary must pay for health-care services or prescriptions, including coinsurance, copayments, and deductibles.

coverage determination (Medicare Part D): A decision made by a Medicare drug plan about whether or not a certain prescription drug is covered under the plan and, if covered, how much a beneficiary must pay.

coverage gap (Part D prescription coverage): A period of time in which you pay higher cost sharing for prescription drugs until you spend enough to qualify for catastrophic coverage. The coverage gap (also called the "donut hole") starts when you and your plan have paid a set dollar amount for prescription drugs during that year.

deductible: The amount you must pay for medical services or prescriptions before your plan begins to pay for your benefits.

exception: A decision by a Medicare drug plan to partially or fully cover the cost of a drug not usually covered by the plan. Exceptions are only issued in special cases and only after receiving a request and medical documentation from a beneficiary who needs the drug.

formulary: A list of drugs your plan covers. Drugs not on the list are not usually covered by the plan.

General Enrollment Period (GEP): If you weren't automatically enrolled in Medicare, and you missed your IEP, you can still apply for Medicare Part A and/or Medicare Part B during the GEP, which runs from January 1 to March 31 each year. If you enroll in Medicare during the GEP, your coverage begins July 1.

grievance: A complaint about the quality of a Medicare health plan or service provider, submitted (in person or in writing) within sixty days of the issue occurring. Beneficiaries can submit grievances based on their satisfaction with care received while in the care of covered providers or the quality of the health plan's service but may not submit grievances about the quality of care at noncovered providers.

guaranteed issue rights: The right to purchase insurance policies that supplement Medicare (known as "Medigap" policies) without being denied or charged more due to preexisting health conditions or past health history.

initial coverage limit (Part D prescription coverage): The annual amount a beneficiary will have to pay for prescriptions (copayments, coinsurance, and deductible combined), beyond which beneficiaries enter the "donut hole" coverage gap.

Initial Enrollment Period (IEP): The seven-month period in which you're first eligible to sign up for Medicare Part A and/or Part B. For example, if you're eligible when you turn sixty-five, your IEP begins three months before the month you turn sixty-five, includes the month you turn sixty-five, and ends three months after the month you turn sixty-five. (We will further illustrate this timing later in the book.)

lifetime reserve days: In Original Medicare, these are additional days that Medicare will pay for when you're in a hospital for more than ninety days. You have a total of sixty reserve days that can be used during your lifetime. For each lifetime reserve day, Medicare pays all covered costs except for the daily coinsurance.

limiting charge: In Original Medicare, the highest amount of money you can be charged for a covered service by doctors and other health-care suppliers who don't accept assignment. The limiting charge is 15 percent over Medicare's approved amount. The limiting charge only applies to certain services and doesn't apply to supplies or equipment.

Medicaid: A state and federal government program that assists people with low income and little money to pay for health-care costs.

medically necessary: Health-care services or supplies that are needed to prevent, diagnose, or treat an illness, injury, condition, disease, or symptoms and that meet accepted standards of medicine.

Medicare Summary Notice (MSN): A notice you get after a doctor, other health-care provider, or supplier files a claim for Part A or Part B services in Original Medicare. It explains what the doctor, other health-care provider, or supplier billed for, the Medicare-approved amount, how much Medicare paid, and what you must pay.

Medicare Supplement (Medigap) Plan: These Medicare-approved health insurance plans are sold by private insurance companies to help cover some or all of the expenses not covered by Medicare Parts A and B. As long as you're eligible, you can apply for a Medicare Supplement Plan at any time during the year.

Medigap open enrollment period (OEP): A single six-month period of time at the beginning of Medicare Part B eligibility, during which laws allow beneficiaries sixty-five and older to purchase any Medigap policy sold in their state, without denial or higher cost due to previous medical issues.

Original Medicare: Medical coverage overseen by the US government, covering hospital insurance with Part A and medical insurance with Part B. Beneficiaries pay a deductible and coinsurance, while Medicare pays for its part of the approved cost of a service or treatment.

prior authorization: Approval that you must get from a Medicare drug plan before you fill your prescription in order for the prescription to be covered by your plan. Your Medicare drug plan may require prior authorization for certain drugs.

service area: A geographic area where a health insurance plan accepts members if it limits membership based on where people live. For plans that limit which doctors and hospitals you may use, it's also generally the area where you can get routine (non-emergency) services. The plan may disenroll you if you move out of the plan's service area.

Special Enrollment Period (SEP): The time during which people can enroll in Medicare Part B if they missed the deadline for enrollment during the IEP because they had coverage at the time through work, a union plan, or a spouse's employer plan.

Special Needs Plan (SNP): A Medicare Part C Advantage Plan that provides coverage to people with specific requirements such as a chronic illness, need for institutional care, or dual eligibility for Medicare and Medicaid.

step therapy: A coverage rule used by some Medicare prescription drug plans that requires you to try one or more similar, lower-cost drugs to treat your condition before the plan will cover the prescribed drug.

Tiers: The classification system used by Medicare Part D drug plans that denotes the out-of-pocket expense (to the beneficiary) of prescription drugs, with tier 1 being the least expensive. Tier 1 drugs are often generic, tier 2 drugs are often name brands, and tier 3 and beyond are usually nonpreferred name brands and specialty prescriptions.

PLEASE

REMEMBER

- ☐ Like everything else, Medicare has its own vocabulary—words, terms, and abbreviations that are all its own.

- ☐ Parts A and B are "Original Medicare."

- ☐ Part A covers the expenses you have if you're in the hospital. In most cases, you don't pay premiums for Part A.

- ☐ Part B covers many outpatient expenses. You have to purchase Part B coverage.

- ☐ Part C is also called "Medicare Advantage." Medicare makes payments to private insurance companies to cover the same things as Parts A and B in addition to some additional benefits.

- ☐ Part D covers prescription drugs.

- ☐ Don't feel as though you need to learn a foreign language before you can understand Medicare. Use this glossary whenever you run into unfamiliar terms.

SIXTY-FIVE—OR OVER

Understanding Enrollment Periods

Recently, while helping with a group medical enrollment for a large company, we met a sixty-eight-year-old gentleman named Gideon. In our discussion with Gideon, he asked us which would be better for him: going on Medicare or with the group plan.

He was amazed when we told him that Medicare would probably be the better choice for him. "How come?" he asked, "No one has ever told me that before."

We explained that Medicare has a lower cost and better benefits than those being offered to him through his employer.

Gideon still looked a little puzzled. "But what about Social Security?" he asked. "Don't I have to start collecting Social Security before I can enroll in Medicare?"

"No, you don't," we explained. "You can apply for Medicare any time once you've turned sixty-five—even if you're still working and covered by your employer health plan."

We went on to spend some more time discussing Social Security with Gideon, since he had many areas of confusion. He was surprised by many of the things we told him. None of it was bad news, though, except that he was a little disappointed in himself for missing out on a few years of benefits to which he was entitled. He decided to make an appointment right away with his local Social Security office.

"I don't know why I waited so long to figure out all these things," he said to us.

"Maybe," we suggested, "because you were putting off thinking about something that made you feel anxious. Sometimes we procrastinate when it comes to the things we're dreading."

"That's it exactly," said Gideon. "The more I procrastinated, the more anxious I felt—and the more anxious I felt, the more I procrastinated. Except, how silly! If I had just found out the facts, I would have realized I didn't have any reason to feel anxious at all. And I would have been better off that much sooner."

We've run into a lot of people who are going through some of the same confusion that Gideon was. He's a smart professional, just like you are—but there was a lot of misinformation and misunderstanding getting in his way. Our job is to help people like Gideon through the whole process so they can make a clear and easy blueprint for their future.

UNDERSTANDING THE ENROLLMENT TIMELINE

There are two main enrollment times for seniors entering into Medicare coverage: the Initial Enrollment Period (IEP) and Special Enrollment Periods (SEPs).

- The IEP is the seven-month period to sign up for Medicare when you turn sixty-five.

- SEPs are specific circumstances when you're allowed to enroll in Medicare Part B, Part C, and/or Part D outside of the IEP or AEP. Most often, SEPs occur when you have stayed on your (or your spouse's) employer group plan and are now planning to leave that plan due to cost, retirement, or personal choice.

By the way, if you have a situation that is different from the two situations we are going to review here (for example, you're not yet sixty-five but are on Medicare due to disability, or you are on both Medicare and Medicaid), please call your local Social Security office for more information. Or give us a call—we'd be happy to help you understand what you need to do.

INITIAL ENROLLMENT PERIOD (IEP)

Your IEP lasts a total of seven months. It begins three months before the month of your sixty-fifth birthday, it includes the month of your birthday, and it extends for three months following the month of your birthday. For example, let's say your birthday is in May. These months would then be your enrollment period:

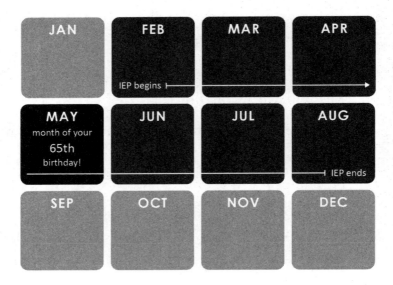

Now let's say you have a December birthday. Then your enrollment period would look like this:

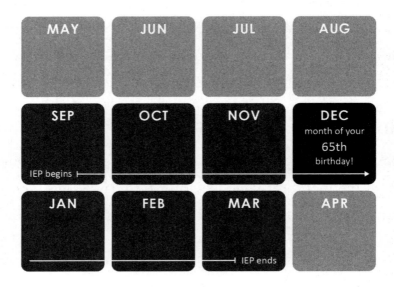

There's no reason not to enroll in Medicare Part A during your seven-month IEP. Depending on your situation, however, you may want to delay enrollment into Part B, due to a variety of situations outlined in the table that follows. In these situations, you will be entitled to an SEP, which we will discuss shortly. Part B has significant, lifelong penalties that can cost you if enrollment is not done properly. In 2017, the monthly cost for Part B is $134 for newly eligible beneficiaries.

Your situation	Should you sign up for Part B during your IEP?	Can you delay Part B at age sixty-five and sign up during an SEP?
You have no other health insurance.	Yes	No
You still work and have group insurance from your employer and intend to keep that coverage.	Yes, if your employer has fewer than twenty full-time employees (Medicare will be primary, and you need to sign up for Part B). No, if your employer has more than twenty full-time employees (unless enrollment in Medicare Part B is required by your employer health plan).	Yes, as long as you are working and eligible for coverage. You have eight months to sign up if you retire or are no longer eligible for employer coverage.
You have individual insurance.	Yes	No

You are covered under COBRA insurance from your work.	Yes	No
You're covered by retiree health benefits from your work.	Yes	No
You have veteran's health benefits from the VA system.	Yes, unless you plan on working and continuing with your employer benefits.	No, unless you plan on working and continuing with your employer benefits.

IEP TIMELINE

Let's use one of our clients, a woman we'll call Jamie, as an example of someone who went on Medicare using the IEP timeline.

Jamie, who came to see us in the summer of 2016, was born on January 12, 1952. This means she will turn sixty-five in January 2017 and will be eligible for Medicare starting then (though her IEP will start in October 2016). Here's the timeline we recommended she follow:

- **July 2016:** Start to review information, like this book and other publications, around six months prior to turning sixty-five to understand your Medicare options.

- **September 2016:** Compare plans that are available. Determine which direction to take for other Medicare benefits: a Medicare Supplement and Part D drug card or a Medicare Advantage Plan. (Later in this book, we will explain the differences and advantages of each.) Then review to see which Medicare Supplement or Medicare Advantage Plan is the best. (This is where Jamie will need to talk with a licensed agent so that she understands not only what she is buying but also which company would be the best choice.)

- **October 2016:** If not starting Social Security income benefits, go online to SSA.gov/Medicare and enroll in Parts A and B of Medicare or enroll at your local Social Security office. If starting Social Security income benefits, we recommend that you set up an appointment with the local Social Security office to apply for Social Security benefits and enroll in Parts A and B of Medicare. Remember: you can only sign up for Medicare through the Social Security Administration, *not* with the Centers for Medicare & Medicaid Services (CMS) or Medicare.gov.

MEDICARE IS HERE FOR YOU

Medicare gives Americans age 65+, and younger individuals with disabilities, an important health safety net.

| 6 MONTHS before your 65th birthday | 4 MONTHS before your 65th birthday | 3 MONTHS before your 65th birthday | 65! |

| Understand your Medicare options. | Compare Medicare plans in your area. | Choose the plan that fits you. |

There was one last thing for Jamie to remember: if she delays signing up for Medicare with Social Security, she will also delay the start of her Part B coverage. If she enrolls during the first three months of her IEP, her coverage will start with the month she's first eligible (January). If she enrolls during the last four months, her coverage will start between one and three months after she enrolls.

This chart outlines when your Medicare Part B becomes effective:

If you enroll at this point in your IEP:	Then your Part B coverage starts:
1 to 3 months before you turn 65	the month you turn 65
the month you turn 65	1 month after enrollment
1 month after you turn 65	2 months after enrollment
2 to 3 months after you turn 65	3 months after enrollment

If you were born on the first of any month, your Medicare start date will not be your birthday month; it will be the month *before* your birthday month. For example, if you were born on March 1, your Medicare coverage will begin February 1.

SPECIAL ENROLLMENT PERIOD (SEP)

Let us suppose that Jamie decided to continue with her (or her spouse's) employer plan and delay Part B enrollment. What happens when she is ready to come off that coverage? Here are two examples of when she can enroll in Part B:

- any time between the end of her IEP at age sixty-five and the time when she (or her spouse) stops work or loses her employer coverage

- up to eight months after this employment or coverage has ended

SEP TIMELINE

Now let's see what Jamie would do if she were to stay on an employer plan for her coverage:

- Jamie is eligible for Medicare starting on January 1, 2017, and she should sign up for Part A during her IEP, assuming that she has worked the required forty work credits (ten years of working and paying the Medicare tax). There is no cost for her to receive Part A coverage.

- If Jamie worked after turning sixty-five and then decided to retire and come off her employer plan, at that point she would qualify for an SEP. Once her employer's coverage ends, Jamie has up to eight months to sign up for her Medicare Part B benefits. Of course, the longer she waits to sign up during this eight-month window, the longer she will be without coverage, since her Medicare coverage will not start until the beginning of the month after she signs up. Jamie could also have signed up for Part B in the month prior to her retirement in order to avoid any time without coverage. Because she already has Part A, she will not be able to enroll online. She will need to call the Social Security Administration at 1-800-772-1213 or contact her local Social Security office to enroll in Medicare Part B coverage.

- At this point, Jamie needs to determine what type of coverage would be best for her and then find the right plan and company for her needs.

QUESTIONS

Jamie's timeline sounds simple when you read it, but we know how confusing it can get when you try to apply it to your own situation. So let's answer some of the questions we hear most often when it comes to enrolling for Medicare Parts A and B:

I am turning sixty-five in three months, and I currently receive my Social Security benefits. What do I do?

If you are already receiving Social Security benefits *before* turning sixty-five, you do not have to do anything. The Social Security Administration will automatically enroll you in Parts A and B. You will receive your red, white, and blue Medicare card in the mail, usually about three months before you turn sixty-five.

If you work for a company with more than twenty full-time employees and are staying on the group insurance plan at work, you usually don't need Part B coverage. If you want to decline Part B, then you will need to follow the instructions that come with your Medicare ID card and send the card back. If you keep the card, you automatically keep Part B and will need to pay the Part B premium. When you come off of the group plan sometime down the road, you will need to sign up for Part B coverage at that time.

We'll discuss penalties later, but for now, know that you will not be penalized for delaying coverage under Part B if you already had "creditable" insurance coverage from an employer after your IEP. Your employer's group coverage will normally be considered creditable coverage. Ask your HR office if you have questions on this. They can tell you if your insurance is creditable or not.

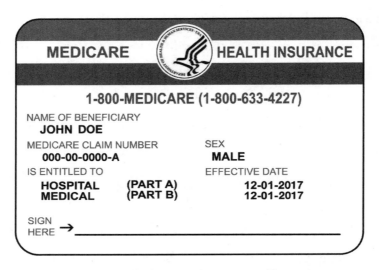

Once you're enrolled in Medicare, you'll receive your red, white, and blue Medicare card in the mail.

I am turning sixty-five in three months, but I am not planning on taking my Social Security benefits yet. What do I have to do? You have some decisions to make. First, though, you should sign up for Medicare. You will need to sign up for Part A. Whether or not you need to sign up for Part B depends on if you're going with Medicare for your coverage or if you're going to stay with your (or your spouse's) employer's group plan.

I am not taking Social Security benefits, and I am going to stay with my employer plan. Now what should I do?

If you are going to stay with your employer plan, that's fine; but you have to determine whether your primary insurance will be Medicare rather than your employer plan. Group plans for employers with fewer than twenty full-time employees will have Medicare as the primary insurance for employees who are sixty-five or older (even if those employees also remain on the employer plan). If this is the case, you will need to sign up for Part B. This is very important because, if you don't sign up for Part B, your employer's group plan will only pay the amount that would have been left after the portion Medicare otherwise would have paid. You'll be responsible for 80 percent of the cost of services covered by Part B.

That is what happened to Fred, who worked at a company with fewer than twenty employees. He didn't sign up for Medicare Part B, because he assumed his employer's insurance would continue to cover him the way it always had. At sixty-seven, Fred had seldom even taken a sick day, and he'd never been hospitalized in his life. A car accident, however, broke both his legs; even after the casts came off, he needed weeks of physical therapy before he could walk normally again. That was bad enough, but then Fred found out that his employer's insurance would only pick up 20 percent of the cost of services because Medicare was now considered his primary insurance *even though he hadn't enrolled in it.* Fred ended up paying a lot of out-of-pocket expenses that he would have avoided if he'd been enrolled in Medicare Part B.

BLUEPRINT TIP

If you're not sure whether your employer has fewer than twenty full-time employees, just ask! If you work for an employer who has more than twenty employees, in most cases, you don't need to sign up for Part B—but ask your employer to be sure.

I am not taking Social Security benefits, because I am waiting for my full retirement age of sixty-six, but I am going to go with Medicare for my insurance coverage.

In this case, you need to sign up for Medicare Parts A and B. There are several ways to do this:

- Make an appointment with your local Social Security office. They will help you sign up for Medicare Parts A and B.

- Go online to sign up for Medicare Parts A and B. It's easy—just go to SSA.gov/Medicare and follow the directions to enroll.

- If you'd like some help, you can call us, and we will walk you through the steps. We can usually get you enrolled in less than ten minutes.

What happens if I don't enroll in Part B during either the IEP or SEP?

If, for whatever reason, you didn't sign up during the seven months of your IEP or the eight-month window of your SEP (if you were eligible), Medicare allows a GEP each year, starting on January 1 and continuing until March 31. During this time, you can sign up for Part B; however, your coverage will not start until July 1 of that year. In most cases, this means that you will be without coverage for an extended period. You will have the option to enroll in an individual plan under the Affordable Care Act (ACA) during the annual OEP (November 1 to January 31). However, if you are eligible for Medicare coverage, you cannot receive a subsidy from the ACA, so you would have to pay the full amount of the premium.

That's what happened to a woman we'll call Patty. When she retired, her employer's COBRA plan extended her insurance for another eighteen months. The eighteen months were up at the end of June, which was when Patty came to us for help applying for Medicare. We were sorry that she hadn't come sooner, because what she hadn't realized was that COBRA doesn't count as employer insurance for Part B enrollment purposes. This meant that she would have to wait until January 1—the beginning of the GEP—before she could apply for Part B coverage, which wouldn't begin until July 1 of that year. This meant that Patty would be without coverage for a full twelve months. We advised her to apply for individual insurance through the ACA, but we knew that the monthly premium was going to take a big bite out of Patty's retirement income.

But we had more bad news to tell Patty. In addition to the delay in coverage, Medicare charges a financial penalty for late enrollments. Her Part B premiums would be 10 percent higher for each full twelve-month period she was without coverage. Worst of all, the penalty is permanent. In other words, she'll be paying that extra 10 percent for as long as she is covered by Medicare Part B. Here is how it works:

- The penalty clock starts at the end of your IEP and continues until the end of the GEP on March 31, even if you signed up in January.

- If you become eligible for Medicare Part B under an SEP, however, then the penalty clock starts at either the time of your retirement or when your group health insurance plan ends (whichever is earlier). Notice that the penalty clock starts at the *beginning* of your SEP, not at the end.

- The 10 percent penalty is calculated as a percentage of the Part B premium and is applied to each month's premium. For example, the Part B premium in 2012 was $99.90 per month. The 10 percent penalty (if, like Patty, you missed only one full twelve-month period) would have added $9.99 to the Part B premium. In

2016, the Part B premium was $104.20, which means the monthly penalty rose to $10.42 per month.

- The "full twelve-month period" means that if you were, for example, thirty months late in signing up for your Part B coverage, you would only have a 20 percent penalty. Medicare would not count the six months between the twenty-fourth month and the thirtieth month, as this is not a "full twelve-month period."

- If you pay more for your Part B coverage due to higher income, the late penalty is applied only to the standard Part B premium. Medicare does not apply the penalty to additional surcharges you pay.

- The penalties can be waived in certain situations. Most of these involve Medicare beneficiaries who are on Medicaid or other assistance programs or who are disabled.

EXAMPLE OF ENROLLMENT PENALTY

Number of Years You Failed to Enroll	Monthly Penalty Increase	Penalty Cost over One-Year Period	Penalty Cost over Five-Year Period	Penalty Cost over Ten-Year Period
1	$13.40	$160.80	$482.40	$964.80
3	$40.20	$482.40	$2,412.00	$4,824.00
5	$67.00	$804.00	$4,020.00	$8,040.00

ENROLLMENT PERIODS FOR OTHER MEDICARE PARTS

Medicare Part C Advantage Plans

Part C, or "Medicare Advantage," plans have the same enrollment period during an IEP and SEP as Original Medicare. Additionally, there is an AEP (October 15 to December 7) during which you can purchase a Medicare Advantage Plan and be guaranteed acceptance. They cannot deny you coverage based on your health history.

Part D

Part D drug coverage has the same enrollment periods as Part C under an IEP or SEP. They also have an AEP like Medicare Part C Advantage Plans.

Medicare Supplement (Medigap) Plans

When you sign up for Part B and you are sixty-five or older, you have a guaranteed window of six months in which to purchase a Medicare Supplement, or "Medigap," policy. This is called the "Medigap OEP." When you are in this guaranteed-acceptance time period, an insurance company cannot turn you down due to your health history. Unlike Medicare Advantage Plans, if you apply for Medigap coverage outside an IEP or SEP, you will have to go through medical underwriting, which means the insurance company will ask you questions about your health history and may turn you down for coverage. It could also accept you for coverage but put up to a six-month preexisting condition limitation on your plan.

PLEASE

- [ ] An IEP is when you are turning sixty-five and sign up for Part B coverage.

- [ ] An SEP is available when you delay signing up for Part B. This is usually due to staying on employer-based coverage.

- [ ] If you delay or forget to sign up for Parts A and B, you can sign up during the GEP. However, this will delay the start of your coverage and may trigger steep, permanent late enrollment penalties.

- [ ] **You may want to discuss with your company's HR department before you make the decision to sign up for Medicare.** They may be able to help you determine what your options are and whether Medicare might be able to offer you more coverage than your employer's health insurance. HR also may be able tell you if your health insurance plan will work differently for you after you sign up for Medicare.

CHAPTER

ORIGINAL MEDICARE

Understanding Hospital and Medical Insurance

We find that many people have the most confusion about how Medicare Parts A and B work and what they cover. In this chapter, we'll explain more about the coverage you'll receive under Parts A and B—what's known as Original Medicare.

PART A

Medicare Part A is usually described as "hospital insurance," a term originally used when Medicare was introduced in 1966. However, this term can be misleading, as Part A doesn't cover everything that happens in a hospital. It does help pay the costs of inpatient care in a hospital or skilled nursing facility, hospice care, and home health care (but not long-term care). Part A could more correctly be called coverage that primarily pays for nursing care. It helps pay for the following:

- nursing services if you're admitted to a hospital or skilled nursing facility or if you qualify for and receive short-term home health services or hospice care in your home

- a semiprivate room in a hospital or nursing facility

- meals provided by a hospital or nursing facility

- services provided by a hospital or nursing facility, like lab tests, prescription medications, medical supplies, and rehabilitation services

- most other costs associated with your stay in a hospital or nursing facility, excluding physician charges

MEDICARE PART A

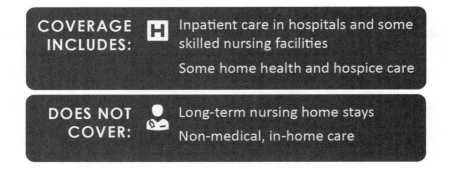

COVERAGE INCLUDES: Inpatient care in hospitals and some skilled nursing facilities

Some home health and hospice care

DOES NOT COVER: Long-term nursing home stays

Non-medical, in-home care

PART B

Medicare Part B, what many call "medical insurance," helps cover doctors' services and outpatient care. It also covers some other medical services that Part A doesn't cover, such as some physical and occupational therapy and some home health care. There is a wide range of other services it covers, including the following:

- physicians' expenses for inpatient and outpatient medical and surgical services

- physical therapy, speech therapy, and diagnostic tests

- clinical laboratory services like blood tests and urinalysis done outside of hospitals and nursing facilities

- many preventive services like flu shots, mammograms, colonoscopies, and so on

- home health-care services like part-time or intermittent skilled care, home health aide services, and durable medical supplies and equipment

- outpatient hospital treatment for the diagnosis or treatment of an illness or injury (e.g., emergency room visits and outpatient surgery)

MEDICARE PART B

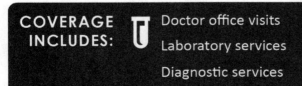

COVERAGE INCLUDES:
Doctor office visits
Laboratory services
Diagnostic services

	Part A	Part B
Premium	$0 for the majority of people. Up to $413 per month if you do not have sufficient work credits, based on your employment record.	$134 per month for newly eligible persons in 2017. There is an additional surcharge (between $53.50 and $294.60 per month) for people with incomes over certain levels. (For more info, see Appendix A.)
Deductible	$1,316 deductible for each sixty-day benefit period (in 2017).	$183 annual deductible (in 2017).
Copayment and coinsurance (See Appendix B for more detailed benefits.)	**Hospital Stays:** Days 1–60: no coinsurance Days 61–90: $329/day Days 91–150: $658/day for each lifetime reserve day Days exceeding 150: all costs **Skilled Nursing Facility Stays:** Days 1–20: zero coinsurance for each benefit period Days 20–100: $164.50/day Days exceeding 100: all costs	You pay 20 percent of *all* costs for Medicare-approved services. The 20 percent is unlimited, unlike most employer plans, which will have a stop-loss provision limiting the total amount you pay.

THE COSTS OF OWNING AND USING YOUR MEDICARE PARTS A AND B INSURANCE

When we talk with people about their options for medical (or any other type of) insurance, we talk about two costs—the cost of *owning* the policy (the premium) and the cost of *using* your coverage (deductibles, copayments, and coinsurance). You need to look at both to make an informed choice about your Medicare options. In the previous chart, you will see the costs for owning and using Parts A and B.

WILL MEDICARE SEND ME INFORMATION ABOUT MY COVERAGE?

A question we hear often is, "Will I get a contract or a certificate of coverage from Medicare for Parts A and B?"

You will not. Unlike individual or group insurance you receive from your employer, when you sign up for Medicare, you don't get a lot of information other than your red, white, and blue Medicare ID card. Many people have questions about what is covered and how they are covered, and there are a number of resources to help them.

The first resource is the official handbook produced by CMS, called *Medicare and You,* which will be mailed to you in the fourth quarter of each year. If you don't have a copy yet, you can go to the Medicare.gov website, scroll to the bottom of the home page, click on "Publications," and either download a copy or have one mailed to you. This publication has a section that is almost forty pages long and reviews a number of conditions and services and how they are covered under Medicare. In our opinion, this guide is well written and informative. However, it can be a bit overwhelming, as it reviews the *entire* Medicare program.

You can also go the Medicare.gov home page, and at the top of the page you will see an area that asks, "Is my test, item, or service covered?" Just type in what you are looking for; it will bring up search results that show a number of pages discussing the answer to your question. In most cases, this will give you the information you need.

If you're not good with computers, you can call Medicare at 1-800-MEDICARE.

DEDUCTIBLES

Many people who are new to Medicare are accustomed to how things worked with their old health insurance, and because of this, when they see the Part A deductible, they think it's something that needs to be met once a year, the same way their old insurance worked. But that's not the way Medicare works. The $1,316 (in 2017) deductible resets sixty days after your release from the hospital or nursing facility. This is called a "benefit period."

Here's how it works. For example, if you were hospitalized on January 1 and released on January 7, but then you were readmitted to the hospital on or before March 8, you would only pay one deductible. However, if you were to go back into the hospital any time after March 8, that would be a new benefit period, and you would be responsible for another $1,316.

The Part B deductible, however, is an annual deductible—like in the insurance we're more accustomed to—so once you meet it for the calendar year, you do not need to satisfy it again during that year.

SKILLED NURSING FACILITIES AND THE "THREE-DAY RULE"

If you have Original Medicare and are admitted to a hospital and then are moved to a Medicare-approved skilled nursing facility, you have to be a patient in the hospital for at least three days for Medicare to pay for services provided by the skilled nursing facility. That sounds pretty straightforward—but sometimes it's not.

It all depends on how you are classified as a patient at the hospital. Are you considered to be an "admitted" patient, or are you under "observation"? Observation status means that the hospital doctors are observing your condition to determine if they should admit you to the hospital or discharge you. Medicare will not count observation days toward the three-day rule. Your doctor will need to write an order for you to be formally admitted as an inpatient for the days to count toward the three-day rule.

Here are other details of the three-day rule:

- The day you are admitted is counted toward the three-day rule, but the day you are discharged is not. In order for a day to be counted, you must be in the hospital at midnight (i.e., the start of the day).

- The three days must be consecutive. If you were admitted on Monday, discharged on Tuesday, and ended up back in the hospital on Thursday, Monday and Tuesday would not count toward the three-day rule. You would need to be a patient in the hospital Thursday, Friday, and Saturday and discharged on Sunday before Medicare would cover any days at a skilled nursing facility.

- While you are under "observation" status, you are considered to be an outpatient, and Part B will pay the charges instead of Part A.

If you (or a family member) are on Medicare and in the hospital, you need to ask what your status is each day you are in the hospital. The hospital can change this status, and they are not obligated to notify you or your family.

What should you do if you're in the hospital "under observation"? You have a few options:

- Ask the hospital doctor to have your case reconsidered or to refer it to the committee that decides status at the hospital.

- Ask your doctor if you can qualify to get similar services under Medicare's home health-care benefit instead of at a skilled nursing facility.

- If you decide that you need to go to a skilled nursing facility and Medicare will not cover it under the three-day rule, you may appeal Medicare's decision.

- If you decide to go to the skilled nursing facility, the SNF must provide you with an ABN that you will need to sign, which explains that you understand you're responsible for the costs of your stay. If they fail to give you the ABN, neither you nor Medicare will be responsible for the charges.

THE MEDICARE BACKBONE

Medicare Parts A and B are the backbone of all Medicare services and provide a broad range of covered services. Most costs are covered under Medicare, and most people who receive Medicare benefits are happy with their coverage. However, there are costs to using the coverage, and it is not structured like most employer or individual plans.

If you travel out of state, your Medicare coverage goes with you. The advantage of Original Medicare is that it is national in scope. Medicare Parts A and B will pay for services that are provided by a Medicare-participating physician or hospital anywhere in the United States. It doesn't matter if the provider is in your state or outside of it. As long as the provider is participating with Medicare, you can see that provider without worry.

WHAT'S NEXT?

While Medicare Parts A and B provide a wide range of benefits and offer very comprehensive insurance coverage, these plans have a few quirks that could potentially cost you a lot of money if you have a major accident or illness.

But there's some good news. The federal government wants seniors to have options to cover these costs, and Medicare has two main ways that let you do this. Medicare has approved numerous private insurance companies to offer options for seniors to remove these risks.

Remember that Medicare Part D is the prescription drug benefit offered under Medicare. We'll devote an entire chapter to it near the end of this book, but for now, understand that Medicare Part D will feel much like the current prescription coverage you may have with your employer plan. There are copays for various medications and (in some cases) a separate deductible to meet. Over the next three chapters, we will simply refer to the Part D plan as something that can either be added to the other plans or is already included in them. After we show you your coverage options, we will follow up with a chapter on the details of Medicare Part D.

UNDERSTANDING YOUR CHOICES

Here are two ways you can make your Medicare coverage the best insurance for your needs:

1. Keep Original Medicare (Parts A and B) and supplement it with a Medicare Supplement (Medigap) Plan and a Part D prescription drug plan.

2. Switch from Original Medicare coverage to a Medicare Part C Advantage Plan. Like Medicare Supplement Plans, these plans are administered by private insurance companies, and the coverage is required to be at least as good as Original Medicare (Parts A and B).

Each of these options offers different advantages and disadvantages. Depending on your needs and concerns, both can be great insurance. However, you need to understand both options in order to make an informed decision. In the next three chapters, we will review these options and show you the pros and cons of each.

PLEASE

☐ Part A's deductible resets sixty days after you are discharged from a hospital or skilled nursing facility (and have not been readmitted). It is not an annual deductible like you probably had with an employer or individual plan.

☐ The Part B deductible is an annual deductible, so you only pay it once per year. Keep in mind, however, that the 20 percent portion of the costs you must pay for is *unlimited*. It does not have an annual or lifetime spending cap like many employer or individual plans.

☐ You will need to pay for all prescriptions unless you purchase a separate Part D drug card. Currently, these plans cost between $15 and $120 per month. Most people find a plan that works for them within the $20 to $50 per month range.

MIND THE GAPS

Understanding Medicare Supplements / Medigap Plans

One of our clients, Susie, visited us, and she had opted to have just Original Medicare (Parts A and B) coverage. Her husband was also sixty-five, and she wanted to make sure he got the coverage he needed because he had a serious medical condition that could reoccur. She also wanted to keep their costs down, though, so she felt that the best solution would be for her to just have Original Medicare.

As we talked to her, we discovered that Susie and her husband have three daughters—two in Florida and one in New York. They travel to see their children several times each year. "Susie," we said, "the best choice for you would be a Medicare Supplement to remove the unlimited out-of-pocket costs you could have with just Original Medicare."

"But what about the cost?" she asked. "I've heard people talk about zero or very low premiums with Medicare Advantage Plans. Would that be an option for me?"

We shook our heads. "Medicare Advantage Plans are limited to providers located within certain geographical locations, such as a county or a state. They use networks of providers to help control their costs. This would not be a good match for your needs because of your frequent travel outside of any single Medicare Advantage Plan's service area."

"So what do you recommend?" Susie asked. We explained that in her case, the high-deductible Plan F (a type of Medigap plan) would be the best choice, as it had the lowest cost of all the standardized plans (less than $50 per month for her, at age sixty-five), and it limited the amount she could owe in any year to $2,200 (as of 2017). This was a lot better than unlimited out-of-pocket costs with just Original Medicare, and it still gave her the flexibility of Original Medicare. In addition, most of the Medicare Advantage Plans in her area cost between $19 and $49 per month, so this plan was comparable in cost while avoiding the network restrictions. Susie nodded and thanked us for introducing her to a great option that she otherwise wouldn't have encountered.

We're glad we could help Susie. The part of this conversation that was disappointing to us was that no other agent had ever discussed this plan with her. This was the first time she had ever heard about Medigap high-deductible Plan F. Knowing all the options that are available can keep you out of situations that could be very costly.

UNDERSTANDING MEDIGAP PLANS

At first, this part of your blueprint may seem a little confusing. You'll hear people talk about Medicare Supplement Plans and Medigap plans. What's the difference between the two?

There isn't any difference, actually. They're the same thing; the terms are used interchangeably, and they refer to the same group of plans that supplement or fill the gaps in Original Medicare. If you look at the wording used by CMS, however, they use the term "Medigap"—so from now on, so will we.

Medigap plans, which are sold by private companies with the approval of CMS, can help pay for some or nearly all of the cost-sharing components that Original Medicare (Parts A and B) doesn't cover, such as deductibles, coinsurance (the 20 percent part we talked about in the last chapter), and copayments. Some Medigap plans also offer coverage for services that are not covered under Original Medicare. Six of the plans offer coverage for medical care when you travel outside the United States. There are also three plans that offer coverage for what are called "excess charges," which we will explain later in this chapter.

HOW DO MEDIGAP PLANS WORK?

Medigap plans do what the name implies—they fill in some or nearly all of the gaps in coverage offered by Original Medicare. The way they work is that your provider (typically a doctor or hospital) files your claim with Medicare; Medicare then reviews the claim, approves it, and pays it. Once Medicare pays the claim, it sends the claim information to your Medigap insurance company, which pays its portion based on the plan you have. Your Medigap insurance company doesn't medically manage these claims. In short, they receive the claim from CMS, and they pay it. If Medicare pays, then they pay. If Medicare doesn't pay for some reason, then the Medigap insurance company won't pay, either.

STANDARDIZED MEDIGAP PLANS

You'll see a lot of information out there about picking one of the ten standardized Medicare Supplement Plans. We're always disappointed when we see information like this, because in our minds, there are *eleven*, not ten standardized plans. However, if you go to Medicare.gov, you will see that even CMS indicates that there are ten standardized Medigap plans.

The plan that they are leaving out can be one of the most important plans for many people. It's the least expensive Medigap plan offered out of all the plans. The plan is called high-deductible Plan F. It has a higher deductible—$2,200 in 2017—but this deductible is relatively small compared to that of many health insurance plans available to individuals, so it can be a viable option for many people. In the following chart, we will include this plan along with the rest.

Medicare Supplement Insurance (Medigap) Plans

BENEFITS	A	B	C	D	F*	G	K	L	M	N
Medicare Part A coinsurance and hospital costs (up to an additional 365 days after Medicare benefits are used)	100%	100%	100%	100%	100%	100%	100%	100%	100%	100%
Medicare Part B coinsurance or copayment	100%	100%	100%	100%	100%	100%	50%	75%	100%	100%***
Blood (first 3 pints)	100%	100%	100%	100%	100%	100%	50%	75%	100%	100%
Part A hospice care coinsurance or copayment	100%	100%	100%	100%	100%	100%	50%	75%	100%	100%
Skilled nursing facility care coinsurance			100%	100%	100%	100%	50%	75%	100%	100%
Part A deductible		100%	100%	100%	100%	100%	50%	75%	50%	100%
Part B deductible			100%		100%					
Part B excess charges					100%	100%				
Foreign travel emergency (up to plan limits)			80%	80%	80%	80%			80%	80%
Out-of-pocket limit in 2017**							$5,120	$2,560		

*Plan F is also offered as a high-deductible plan by some insurance companies in some states. If you choose this option, this means you must pay for Medicare-covered costs (coinsurance, copayments, deductibles) up to the deductible amount of $2,200 in 2017 before your policy pays anything.

**For Plans K and L, after you meet your out-of-pocket yearly limit and your yearly Part B deductible ($183 in 2017), the Medigap plan pays 100% of covered services for the rest of the calendar year.

*** Plan N pays 100% of the Part B coinsurance, except for a copayment of up to $20 for some office visits and up to a $50 copayment for emergency room visits that don't result in an inpatient admission.

These are the standardized Medigap plans, which are denoted by the letters A through N. Each plan will be exactly the same regardless of the private insurance company offering it (all Plan Fs will be the same, all Plan Gs will be the same, and so on). By law, companies must offer the same benefits.

PART B EXCESS CHARGES

While many people and some insurance agents either don't know or don't talk much about "excess charges," this coverage can be important. Many physicians and hospitals accept what Medicare pays for approved services. This is called "assignment," and providers who accept Medicare patients on assignment can't charge more than the Medicare-approved amount for their services. However, there are providers who accept Medicare patients but do not accept assignment of Medicare. In these cases, they can see Medicare patients, but they are limited in how much they can charge for their services. This is what is called the "limiting charge." Non-assignment providers are limited to charging no more than 15 percent above the Medicare-approved amount. Medicare will pay for its portion (80 percent) of the approved amount, but the beneficiary is responsible for the full amount of "excess charge" (plus the standard 20 percent coinsurance of the approved amount).

Martha, for example, was visiting her children, just as she does each year. She normally sees her long-time physician at home for her care. However, she had the flu while she was away from home, so she went for an office visit with a physician who accepts Medicare patients but does not take assignment from Medicare. Martha has Original Medicare (Parts A and B) along with Medigap Plan F.

Let's assume that the Medicare-allowed charge for Martha's visit was $100. The physician has the option (and the right) to charge up to 15 percent more than the Medicare-approved amount (the limiting charge). In this example, the physician Martha saw can charge an additional $15 and bill a total of $115 for her visit. Medicare Part B would pay $80 (80 percent of the Medicare-allowed charge of $100). Martha's Medigap Plan F would then pay the remaining 20 percent, as normal. Because Medigap Plan F covers "excess charges," it would also pay the additional $15.

Now imagine that Martha came down with something much worse than the flu and needed $5,000 in Medicare-allowed services from that same non-assignment doctor. The doctor could charge up to $750 extra. If Martha *didn't* have Medigap Plan F, she would be responsible for that $750 plus the usual 20 percent of the Medicare-allowed charge ($1,000) for a total of $1,750. As you can see, these things add up fast.

The main point here is that if you need to see providers who don't accept Medicare assignment, you can see them, but the cost will be higher. However, Medigap Plan F, high-deductible Plan F, or Plan G (and only these three plans) will pay the additional 15 percent above the Medicare-approved amounts that is charged by nonparticipating doctors. This means that these plans pay the 20 percent coinsurance of Medicare Part B *and* the entire (up to 15 percent) excess charge if you see a doctor who does not take Medicare assignment.

We like these three plans, both because of this benefit and because of their potential value in a future where Medicare may change its benefits. In our opinion, for Medicare to remain financially solvent, it will have to either secure additional government funding or take measures to reduce or freeze the amounts it pays to doctors and hospitals. If those cuts are made, having one of these three Medigap plans will give you a greater chance of being seen by your current doctors, even if they stop seeing most Medicare-eligible patients as a result of these possible cuts. This is because with Medigap, physicians know that you will be able to pay the maximum allowed under the Medicare guidelines. It's not a guarantee they will see you, but it gives you a chance to maintain your relationship with your existing doctors.

You may only have one chance to pick a Medigap plan that covers Part B excess charges. This is why we usually only recommend Plan F, high-deductible Plan F, or Plan G (and why we don't recommend Plan N as often). You need a plan that will work for you both now and in the future.

Here are a few more details about Medigap plans:

- **You will need to have Medicare Parts A and B in order to purchase a Medigap plan.**

- **There will be a separate premium for the Medigap plan in addition to the premium you pay for Medicare Part B.**

- **Medigap plans are individual coverage, meaning that each person will need his or her own plan**. Many companies offer discounts if you are either married or if both you and your spouse are on the same insurance company's plans. These are called "household" discounts, and they can range from 5 percent to about 12 percent off the normal premium costs.

- **Current Medigap plans do not cover prescription medication that you get at your local pharmacy or by mail order.** If you need this coverage, then you have to purchase a separate Part D prescription drug plan (and we recommend you do).

- **You cannot have a Medigap plan and a Medicare Advantage Plan at the same time.**

- **Medigap plans are "guaranteed renewable" regardless of how many claims you have under the plan.** This means the insurance company can't cancel your Medigap policy as long as you pay the premium.

- **Medigap plans automatically renew each year, and the insurance company cannot change any of the benefits in the plan.** However, CMS will periodically add, modify, or delete plans as they deem necessary. The last time there were changes to the standardized plans was 2010. You won't need to review your Medigap coverage each year, as your benefits won't change. However, you will normally have an annual increase in the cost of your plan and need to be aware of those changes. Your insurance company is required by CMS to provide you advance notice of any changes to your premium amount.

QUESTIONS

We know this part of your blueprint is a little complicated. Here are the questions we hear most often when it comes to Medigap plans:

Are there items not covered by a Medigap plan?

Medigap plans only pay for Medicare-approved services. Again, if Medicare pays for it, then your Medigap plan will pay the remaining coinsurance, deductible, or copayment (depending on the plan). But Medigap doesn't cover all services:

- It doesn't offer coverage for long-term care, such as that you would receive in a nursing home.

- It doesn't offer coverage for vision, dental care, or hearing aids.

- It doesn't cover private-duty nursing.

When is the best time to purchase a Medigap plan?

The very best time to purchase a Medigap policy is during your Medigap OEP. This is a six-month window that begins on the first day of the month in which you're sixty-five or older *and* enrolled in Medicare Part B. During this period, an insurance company cannot use medical underwriting. This means that if you have an ongoing health problem, the insurance company can't refuse to sell you any Medigap plan it offers and can't charge you more than they would charge someone with no health problems.

Your Medigap OEP rights depend on when you choose to enroll in Medicare Part B. If you're sixty-five or older, your Medigap OEP begins when you enroll in Part B. This is a one-time-only situation. In most cases, it makes sense to enroll in Part B and purchase a Medigap plan when you are first eligible for Medicare. For most people, this will be when they turn sixty-five. However, there are exceptions if you have employer coverage. (See Appendix C for other enrollment periods, called "Guaranteed Issue Rights.")

What happens if I have employer group coverage?

If you have decided to continue with your (or your spouse's) employer coverage, then you may wait to enroll in Part B. As we explained in chapter 3, unless you work for an employer with fewer than twenty employees, you will not normally be required to have Part B coverage, and you would be paying for it before you need it. Please verify this with your employer. When you decide to end coverage with your (or your spouse's) employer plan, then you will have a chance to enroll in Part B without a late enrollment penalty. Once enrolled in Part B, you can take advantage of your six-month Medigap OEP and choose any Medigap plan offered by the insurance company of your choice, without having to answer any questions about your health.

What if I work for a small company with fewer than twenty employees?

If your employer has fewer than twenty employees, the group insurance plan will be "secondary" and your Medicare will be "primary." This means that Medicare will pay your claims first, and your employer plan will pay after Medicare pays. In this case, your employer plan is effectively acting like a Medigap plan. Your employer carrier will receive the claims from CMS and pay its portion based on the plan you have.

Remember, though—if your company has fewer than twenty employees, you need to sign up for Part B as soon as you turn sixty-five. If you haven't enrolled in Part B coverage, then you may end up paying the 80 percent that Medicare "would have paid," and the group plan will pay only the remaining 20 percent. Obviously, this is not what you want to happen!

In cases like this, if you did take Part B coverage at age sixty-five (because you had to in order to have full coverage under the "secondary" employer group coverage), you would have a Medigap SEP when your employer plan ends. You can enroll in a Medigap plan during this SEP, and you do not have to answer any health questions. It doesn't matter *why* your employer plan ends; you might decide to end the plan with your employer, you might no longer be eligible for coverage due to retirement or a reduction in hours, or the employer might terminate the plan. In all these cases, your Medigap SEP will begin once the plan ends.

Is there any difference between the Medigap OEP and an SEP?

The major difference between a Medigap OEP and an SEP is that with an SEP, you are limited to choosing only Medigap Plans A, B, C, F, K, and L. With the Medigap OEP, you can choose any of the eleven Medigap plans offered.

What happens if I want to change plans after a few years?

With a Medigap plan, you can choose to change to a different Medigap plan at any point during the year. If you are outside of your Medigap OEP, however, in the majority of situations, you will have to go through "medical underwriting"—in other words, the insurance company can look at your health conditions to determine if it wants to accept you for coverage. They may decide to limit your coverage to exclude preexisting health conditions that you've had for up to six months. If you had a serious health issue like an internal cancer or a heart attack within the last five years, or you are currently in treatment for some other serious condition, you most likely will not be approved for coverage.

However, each insurance company will have slightly different underwriting guidelines, and a knowledgeable agent can call the insurance companies and predetermine if your condition could qualify for coverage. In many cases, if you have been clear of treatment for two to five years, you may be able to move to a different insurance company. In Appendix D, there is a sample of the "typical" medical questions that are asked. If you can say no to all of the questions, then you may be able to switch plans. We have had situations where we were able to provide additional information to the underwriting department and get an individual approved. Remember, it doesn't cost anything but your time to see if you can switch.

Why would I choose a Medigap plan in the first place?

There are specific reasons why a Medigap plan might be a better choice than a Medicare Advantage Plan, but it is always based on what your needs are and what is important to you. Here are some of the major reasons why someone might choose a Medigap plan:

- *You want to keep your current doctor(s).* Medigap plans do not have a "network" of participating physicians. You are free to use any Medicare-participating physician. Most physicians and nearly all hospitals participate with Medicare.

- *The Medigap insurance company can't deny coverage of any medical services, so long as Medicare approves them.* Your Medigap insurance plan simply follows what Medicare does; if a charge is approved, the Medigap insurance company will pay its portion based on the plan you have.

- *You don't want to be surprised with large medical bills.* One advantage of Medigap plans is that you have a choice of plans, from high-deductible plans to one that covers nearly all the gaps in Original Medicare. The high-deductible Plan F has the highest deductible ($2,200), and Plan K has the highest out-of-pocket limit ($5,120). The "regular" Plan F offers nearly 100 percent coverage of the gaps in Original Medicare, and Plan G covers everything Plan F does except for the Part B deductible ($183). So you can pick a plan that offers you little or no out-of-pocket costs, and you won't have any unexpected medical bills.

- *You want a plan that's easy to work with and doesn't have to be renewed every year.* Medigap plan benefits will not normally change year to year, and as long as you pay the premium, they cannot be canceled. They are easy to manage because the only part that normally changes is the premium.

How do I choose between all the companies offering Medigap plans?

One of the things we hear often is that because Medigap plans are "all the same," buying the least-expensive plan would make the most sense. Why would you pay more for a Plan F from *x* insurance company than from *y* insurance company? Well, if all things were equal, we would agree with you. However, insurance companies are not all the same, even if the benefit plan is the same. What you need to do, in our opinion, is ask the following questions:

- How stable is the company you are considering?

- What are its financial ratings?

- What is its history of rate increases over the last four to five years?

- What are its scheduled increases in premiums due to increases in age over the next few years?
- How long has it been in business?
- What is its share of the market, and how profitable is the business it already has?

You should ask these types of questions to ensure that you sign up with a company that is stable and will have only modest premium increases as you get older. While there is no guarantee that a company's recent premium trends will predict its premium increases in the future, it is sensible to look at these areas to give yourself the best chance of avoiding unpleasant surprises.

When we sit with clients to review their Medigap options, we have an online tool that allows us to answer the previous questions. We can look at each company and see its financial ratings, its rate increase history, the rate increases it has in place as you get older, and how profitable its current business is. This gives us a factual basis for evaluating each insurance company. We don't want you to spend more than you need to for coverage, but we do want you to have coverage from a stable, financially secure insurance company. In most cases, we look for larger insurance companies with a proven track record of stable rates.

The good news is that there are well over a hundred companies selling Medigap plans in the United States. This allows you to pick from a number of insurance companies in your area and evaluate them based on facts to make sure you choose the best plan for you. The online tool that we use is widely available, and insurance agents who specialize in Medigap plans should also have this information available.

PLEASE

REMEMBER

Most people who choose a Medigap plan do so for the following reasons:

☐ Medigap plans provide freedom to use any doctor who accepts Medicare, whether they take "assignment" or not.

☐ Medigap plans have a wide choice of coverage options, and a few of them will cover all or nearly all of the cost-sharing portions of Original Medicare. The most popular plans, in our experience, are Plan F, then Plan G, followed by Plan N. When people understand the high-deductible Plan F option, many find it to be a viable option as well.

☐ With Medigap plans, it is important that you understand the proper time to enroll so that you can bypass medical underwriting. It doesn't mean that you can't change to a different Medigap plan later. However, you may not have that option if you have an ongoing health condition in the future.

☐ Picking a plan can be easy; picking the right insurance company to administer your plan is the most-important decision. Choosing the least-expensive plan is not usually the best choice.

☐ Six of the Medigap plans offered have coverage for emergency services provided when you are outside of the United States. If you travel internationally, this may be a valuable benefit.

☐ Three of the Medigap plans (F, G, and HDF) offer coverage for "excess charges."

MEDICARE ADVANTAGE

Understanding Medicare Part C

Joanne works for one of our clients who, at one time, offered a group health plan for its employees. However, in 2012, the costs for this coverage became too much for the employer to fund. But Joanne was sixty-two at the time, and if you have ever looked at the rates for individual coverage at this age, you will know why she couldn't afford it. It wasn't until the adoption of the ACA in 2014 that we were able to get coverage for her (with a sizeable subsidy).

Joanne works hard, but the textile industry is not a high-paying field, and she makes less than $20,000 per year. When she turned sixty-five last year, we discussed her options with Medigap plans and Medicare Part C Advantage Plans. The Medigap options were appealing, but for her, the cost was prohibitive. The high-deductible Plan F had an acceptable monthly cost, but she did not have the resources to handle the higher deductible. So we looked at the Medicare Advantage Plans available to her in her county.

The first thing to see was if her current physician was participating with any of the plans. Fortunately, that physician was participating in one of the available Advantage Plans. This plan also included prescription drug coverage, so we then looked at the medications she was taking. She was only on two medications, both were generics, and they were both covered under the plan. This plan also had a $15 copayment for her primary care physician and a $50 copayment for specialists. If she had to be admitted to the hospital, her cost would be $395 per day, limited to six days of charges. Her out-of-pocket cost was limited to $6,700 per year, but that was better than an unlimited out-of-pocket potential if she only had Original Medicare.

Additionally, she wanted access to physician services. The office visit copayments were something she could afford. The cost for the plan was $39 per month in 2016 (it went to $36 in 2017), so that was also affordable. The other aspect of the plan that she liked was that she didn't need a referral to see a specialist. Her plan is a preferred provider organization (PPO), which means she can go to see any physician, even if they don't participate with the plan. If she did go to a nonparticipating physician, her costs might be higher, but it's nice to have that option if a serious health condition arises. The Medicare Part C Advantage Plan was and still is the best choice for her.

UNDERSTANDING MEDICARE PART C ADVANTAGE

Medicare Part C Advantage Plans, often called "Advantage Plans" or "Advantage-PD Plans," are administered by private insurance companies under the supervision and approval of CMS, which manages the Medicare program. "Advantage-PD" means the plan includes prescription drug coverage. Unlike a Medigap plan that supplements Original Medicare, these plans transfer Original Medicare (Parts A and B) to a third-party insurance company or replace it entirely. Medicare pays the insurance company a flat rate per month (based on the average cost for Original Medicare per person, by county), and the insurance company builds a health plan to help pay for your care.

Remember that these insurance companies must follow the rules set by Medicare. Medicare Advantage Plans are network-based plans that work similarly to many employer or individual insurance plans.

Here are some key facts about Medicare Advantage Plans:

- You must continue to pay the Part B premium in order to have an Advantage Plan.
- You must live in the service area in which the plan is offered.
- Advantage Plans are required to cover all the services covered by Medicare Parts A and B.

- These plans will have a network of physicians and other providers who participate in the plan.

- These plans will typically have copayments for services like office visits or inpatient hospital stays. They may also have a coinsurance percentage that you would be responsible for, such as 20 percent of the cost of an MRI, for example. In Appendix B, we have provided an example of the benefits offered by one plan for your review.

- Unlike Medigap plans, which are standardized, Advantage Plans can and will have different copayments and out-of-pocket limits, as well as different rules on how you get services (such as whether you need to have a referral to see a specialist).

- Advantage Plans will have an out-of-pocket cost limit ($6,700 is the highest possible cost limit in 2017), unlike Original Medicare, which does not have such a limit.

- Advantage Plans often have built-in Medicare prescription drug coverage (Part D).

- There are low-premium and possibly even zero-premium Advantage Plans.

- These plans cannot refuse to provide you coverage based on any preexisting condition or health history.

The only exception is if you have kidney failure (end-stage renal disease).

- Advantage Plans may have additional benefits not covered under Original Medicare. Benefits like dental, vision, and hearing services may be included with your coverage.

- Medicare Advantage Plans must be renewed each year, as they can have changes in benefits, provider networks, and cost.

- You cannot have a Medicare Advantage Plan and a Medigap plan at the same time. You can only have one or the other—not both.

Just like Original Medicare, Medicare Advantage Plans cover emergency or urgent care service throughout the United States.

QUESTIONS

Just as with all the other parts of your Medicare blueprint, we find that people have lots of questions about Medicare Advantage Plans. Here are some of the most common.

When can I join or switch to another Medicare Advantage Plan?

Like Medigap plans, you can join a Medicare Advantage Plan when you first become eligible for Medicare during your IEP or if you qualify for an SEP. Unlike Medigap plans, you can also join or switch coverage to another Medicare Advantage Plan during the AEP that occurs from October 15 to December 7. Your coverage would then begin on January 1.

What are the most important considerations in choosing a Medicare Advantage Plan?

There are two things you must do to determine if a specific Medicare Advantage Plan is right for you:

- **Make sure the physicians you want to see are participating in the plan.** If you chose a plan that your physician does not participate in, you may have to pay a higher cost to see that physician. In many areas of the country, there are dozens of companies offering these plans, so you may have a number of network options to choose from.

- **Check to see if your prescription drugs are covered under the plan.** All Advantage Plans will provide a list of covered medications (a formulary) that will show if they are covered and what "tier" the medications will be under (this determines the copayment you are charged). We believe this is the single most important consideration in choosing an Advantage Plan.

What are the different types of Medicare Advantage Plans?

There are a number of different types of Medicare Advantage Plans offered in the United States. The two most popular are the following:

- Health Maintenance Organization (HMO)
- Preferred Provider Organization (PPO)

These are the major differences between the two plans:

- With an HMO plan, you will normally be limited to seeing only physicians and other providers who are participating with the plan. They must be "in-network" in order for the plan to pay for their services. If they are not participating, then you will be responsible for the full costs of the services provided.

- With a PPO plan, you will also have a network of providers and physicians for whom you would only pay the copayment, as you would with an HMO plan. If you want to see a physician who does not participate with the plan, you can do so, and unlike an HMO, a PPO will cover some of these "out-of-network" costs. However, the insurance company will not limit the amount that the out-of-network provider can charge you. The Advantage Plan usually will pay nonparticipating physicians just as if they were participating physicians, but those physicians can require you to pay the difference between what they charge and what the Advantage Plan pays. This is called "balance billing"; the PPO pays part of the costs, and you pay the "balance."

Most HMO plans will require you to pick a primary care physician and will require a referral to see a specialist. Most PPO plans do not require a primary care physician or referrals to see a specialist.

Make sure that your HMO or PPO plan covers prescriptions. If it does not, you will need to purchase a separate Part D prescription drug plan. Most PPO plans will have prescription drug coverage, but you need to make sure.

What are Special Needs Plans (SNPs)?

SNPs are available for people in the following situations:

- People who live in institutions like nursing homes, who require nursing services at home, or both.

- People who, due to low income, are eligible for both Medicaid and Medicare (these are called "dual eligible" plans).

- People who have specific, chronic conditions like diabetes, HIV/AIDS, chronic heart failure, or dementia.

Because of the complexity of these plans, they are outside the scope of this book. We could easily spend dozens of pages on these plans. In our experience, though, if you qualify for a SNP, it can be an excellent choice for coverage. Please do not overlook these plans if you think you might qualify.

Medicare.gov offers a booklet that explains these options in greater detail, and it's well done. Just go to Medicare.gov, scroll to the bottom of the home page, and click on "Publications." When the next page opens, enter "Your Guide to Medicare Special Needs Plans (SNPs)" in the search field. Please make sure to type in the title completely or your search may come back empty.

Why would I choose a Medicare Advantage Plan?

Medicare Advantage Plans can be a great choice for coverage for many people, depending on their needs. Some of the reasons to choose a Medicare Advantage Plan are as follows:

- **Advantage Plans can be an affordable choice**, as there are usually low-cost, or in some cases zero-premium, options available. This can be an important feature, especially if you're on a fixed income.

- **They usually include prescription coverage,** which means you won't have to purchase a separate Part D drug card.

- **They offer a cap or limit on the out-of-pocket costs you can incur,** which is an advantage over Original Medicare, which does not limit your out-of-pocket costs.

- **Medicare Advantage Plans may also offer additional benefits** that are not included in Original Medicare.

Remember that prior to joining a plan, you *must* make sure that your current prescriptions are covered by the plan and that the physician(s) you want to see are participating providers.

MEDICARE ADVANTAGE PLANS AND INSURANCE AGENTS

CMS has very strict guidelines for the marketing of Advantage Plans. This is because in the past, overzealous agents used high-pressure tactics to persuade seniors to sign up for these plans. Although Advantage Plans can be excellent insurance, your particular needs should always come first. No matter how great the plans or the company offering them, they are not right for everybody. If you are interested in looking at a Medicare Advantage Plan, please keep in mind the following guidelines:

- Insurance agents cannot cold call you on the phone in regards to an Advantage Plan. You need to make the initial contact with the agent or company.

- Once you make this initial contact, the agent is required to send you what is called a "Scope of Appointment" letter for any appointment you schedule with the agent. This letter will ensure that your appointment focuses on only the products you are interested in. On the form, you can indicate the product(s) that you want to look at, such as a Medicare Advantage Plan, a Part D drug card, and/or a dental plan.

- Agents are required to wait at least two days before they can meet with you.

- Agents are not allowed to discuss or sell you a non-health-related product (like an annuity or life insurance) when they are talking to you about a Medicare health or drug plan. If you want to look at these products, you will need to set up a separate appointment.

PLEASE

REMEMBER

☐ Medicare Advantage Plans offer an alternative to Original Medicare and can be an excellent option for many people.

☐ To get the most out of your Advantage Plan, make sure to review its network of providers to see if the physicians you want to see participate with the plan.

☐ Check the plan's prescription drug formulary to be sure that your medications are covered.

☐ Medicare Advantage Plans can change and normally do so (to some extent) each year. These changes typically include changes to network providers, covered prescription medications, copays, coinsurance, deductibles, and out-of-pocket maximums. You will need to review your plan every year to make sure it's still a good choice for you.

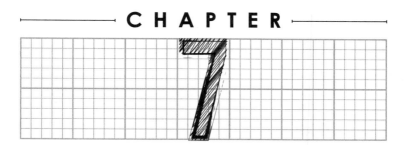

THE COST OF MEDICATIONS

Understanding Part D Prescription Drug Plans

Ellyn enrolled herself in a Medicare Part D plan prior to meeting with our agency. She had a serious preexisting condition and was concerned, as she had expensive prescriptions and didn't want to miss signing up for coverage. She had received information in the mail about what sounded like a good plan at a good price, so she had signed up. However, what she hadn't realized was that her brand name medications were not covered by that plan. She didn't know to check the formulary (the list of medications covered by the plan).

We sat down with Ellyn to review her options. Luckily, we were able to move her to a Medicare Part D plan that covered her medications, reducing her out-of-pocket costs by over $5,300.

We were thankful that we had spoken with her in time so that she could switch plans to one that made sense for her. If she had waited another month, she would have had to wait until the next AEP started on October 15, which was seven months later. It was a close call!

PART D DRUG CARDS

Part D, often called the "Medicare prescription drug benefit," is a federal program to subsidize the costs of prescription drugs and prescription drug insurance premiums for individuals on Medicare. Part D was enacted as part of the Medicare Modernization Act of 2003 and went into effect on January 1, 2006. Original Medicare (Parts A and B) does not cover prescription drugs, so Part D was developed to help pay these costs. While this is a federal program, private insurance companies administer all Part D plans.

PART D PAYMENT LEVELS

Part D prescription plans all have four levels or stages:

- **Level 1 is the annual deductible level**. By law, the highest the deductible can be is $400 (in 2017). However, there are a number of plans that offer coverage without a deductible. If the plan you choose has a deductible, you must pay the annual deductible before the plan will start paying for your prescription medications.

- **Level 2 is called the "initial coverage level."** If your medication is covered, then you pay the copayment or coinsurance percentage for the type of medication (generic, preferred brand name, or nonpreferred brand name). Each plan will have slightly different copayments and coinsurance amounts, and it is extremely important to know if your medication is on the formulary. If your plan doesn't cover a medication you are taking, then you need to select a different plan that does.

- **Level 3 is the coverage gap or the "donut hole."** Most people don't reach this level. It is based on the total cost of your medications (the part you pay plus the part the insurance company pays).

- **Level 4 is the "catastrophic coverage stage."** For people who have reached this level, the cost for medications is highly subsidized so that their costs are greatly reduced.

In the Part D system, prescription medications are divided into up to five different tiers, including generic, brand name, and specialty medications (usually injectable drugs). When you look at the formulary to make sure your prescription medication is covered, there will be a tier level (1 to 5) indicated next to the medication. This will show you the copayment or coinsurance amount for that medication.

MEDICARE PART D

| Annual Deductible | Initial Coverage Level | Donut Hole "Gap" | Catastrophic Coverage |

| $0 | $400 | AFTER DEDUCTIBLE | $3,700 | $4,950 |

If your plan has a deductible, you will pay the full cost of your prescriptions until you reach the deductible amount set by your plan. After the deductible has been reached, you move into the initial coverage level.

Initial Coverage Level	Coverage Gap or "Donut Hole"	Catastrophic Coverage
Your cost is either a copayment or a percentage of the cost of the medication, depending on your plan (most have copayments). Your insurance company pays the rest of the cost for the medication. You will stay in this level until your total medication costs reach $3,700. (All plans are based on a calendar year.)	After your total medication costs reach $3,700, you will pay • 40% of the cost of a brand name medication. • 51% of the cost of a generic medication. You will stay in this level until your total medication costs reach $4,950.	After your total medication costs reach $4,950, you will pay a small copayment or coinsurance amount for prescription drugs. For most medications, the copayment or coinsurance will be $3.30 for generics, $8.25 for brand names, or 5% of the total cost, whichever is greater. You will stay in this level for the remainder of the year.

These items count toward the coverage gap:

- your yearly deductible, coinsurance, and copayments
- the discount you get on brand name drugs in the coverage gap
- what you pay in the coverage gap

These items *don't* count toward the coverage gap:

- the drug plan premium
- pharmacy dispensing fees
- what you pay for drugs that aren't covered
- the discount you get on generic drugs in the coverage gap

THE PART D LATE ENROLLMENT PENALTY

As with Part B, if you don't sign up for a Part D drug card when you are first eligible, there will be a penalty based on how long you were without coverage.

To calculate the penalty, Medicare starts with the "national base beneficiary premium" (i.e., the base monthly cost of a Part D drug card, which is $35.63 in 2017). Medicare multiplies 1 percent of the national base beneficiary premium times the number of full months you didn't have Part D or other creditable prescription coverage (such as a group plan from an employer). The monthly penalty is rounded to the nearest $0.10 and added to your monthly Part D premium.

Here is an example of how the penalty works. When we talked with Susan about Medicare Part D, we found that because she was in good health, she hadn't felt that she needed to enroll in a Part D drug card when she had turned sixty-five. "After all," she said, "I didn't take any prescription medicines, and I never had. How was I to know?"

Unfortunately, about a year and a half after her sixty-fifth birthday, Susan developed a condition requiring medications that cost about $200 per month. She was diagnosed in November of that year and was able—luckily—to sign up for a Part D drug card during the AEP (October 15 to December 7).

She was dismayed when we explained to her that because she had been without coverage for nineteen months before signing up for Part D, her penalty was $6.80 per month ($35.63 × 0.01

X 19 months = $6.77, rounded to $6.80). She hadn't realized there was a penalty or that the penalty was permanent. In addition, because the average cost for a Part D drug card usually increases slightly year to year, the penalty will also increase.

We wish we could have talked to Susan sooner. If we had, she could have taken the least expensive Part D drug card offered when she first enrolled, and it would have cost her about $16 per month. Unfortunately, she will have to pay this penalty for the rest of her life.

QUESTIONS

When people like Susan come to talk to us about Part D coverage, here are some of the common questions we hear:

How do Part D drug cards control costs?

People ask us all the time why one drug card is more expensive than another one. The obvious answer is that the more expensive one will cover more medications (have a larger formulary). While this may be the case, there are other ways for Part D plans to control costs, which may result in a lower premium for the beneficiary. Part D plans use the following methods to manage costs:

- **Prior authorization***:* Your plan may require this for certain prescriptions. This means that before the plan covers a certain medication, your physician will need to show that the medication is "medically necessary."

Plans do this so they can be sure a medication is being used correctly. "Prior auth," as it's called, will cause some disruption, as it will usually require a letter or phone call from your physician or physician's office in order to get your medication covered. If you see this limitation on any of your medications, you should talk with your physician before going to the pharmacy to pick up your medication. Without the prior authorization, the pharmacy won't be able to fill your prescription under the Part D drug card.

- **Step therapy:** This means that before your plan covers a specific medication, it will ask you to try a less expensive, covered drug that is used for the same or similar condition. You may have already done this, as most physicians will try to keep costs down by prescribing a generic or lower-cost brand name medication. If your plan requests this and your physician feels you need the more expensive medication, your physician or physician's office will need to contact your plan to request an exception. If your exception is approved, the plan will cover the more expensive medication. You can also write a formal appeal to your plan if you disagree with its decision.

- **Quantity limits:** Due to safety reasons and to help control costs, your plan may put quantity limits on your medication. The obvious example is a narcotic medication given for pain, but there are other situations that can lead to quantity limits. If your physician feels that the limitation is not appropriate for your condition, you or your physician can contact the plan and ask for an exception. If approved, the plan will remove the limitation for the rest of the year.

Not all pharmacies participate with all the insurance companies offering Part D coverage. Nearly all of the major chains will participate with most of the plans, but some smaller, local pharmacies may not. You need to review this before signing up for Part D if using your current pharmacy is important to you.

How do I get started?

If you're a do-it-yourself type of person, you can go to Medicare. gov and see all the available plans in your county. While the Medicare.gov website is excellent, it can be confusing at first. To get to the relevant page, just go to Medicare.gov. On the left-hand side of the home page, there will be a green box that says "Find health & drug plans." Click on this icon, and it will redirect you to the Medicare Plan Finder. On the right-hand side of this page, you'll see a box that says "Step by step overview on how to complete a plan search." This short video (less than five minutes) will walk you through the entire process. Remember to write down your "Drug List ID and Password Date" when you enter your medications so you won't need to reenter all your medications if you want to go back in to review your options.

If you would rather have someone else get this information for you, that's not a problem. Just call or e-mail us your information (a list of current medications with the exact name on the prescription container, the dosage, the quantity per month, and the name of your preferred pharmacy), and we will go into Medicare.gov and set up the plan finder for you. We will then send you the link, drug list ID, and password date so that you can access the results and review your options. We can review these with you—and there is no charge for this service!

Do I have to pay more for a Part D drug card if I have a high income?

Just like with your Part B premium, if you have an income over a certain level, you will have to pay an Income-Related Monthly Adjustment Amount (IRMAA) in addition to the Part D plan premium. This chart shows the levels and costs:

Your filing status and yearly MAGI income in 2015 (See Appendix A)			Amount you pay each month
Individual tax return	Married, joint tax return	Married, separate tax returns	
$85,000 or less	$170,000 or less	$85,000 or less	Your plan premium
Above $85,000 up to $107,000	Above $170,000 up to $214,000		$13.30 + your plan premium
Above $107,000 up to $160,000	Above $214,000 up to $320,000		$34.20 + your plan premium
Above $160,000 up to $214,000	Above $320,000 up to $428,000	Above $85,000 up to $129,000	$55.20 + your plan premium
Above $214,000	Above $428,000	Above $129,000	$76.20 + your plan premium

If you have to pay an IRMAA, Medicare will either take this out of your Social Security check or will send you a bill (if you're not taking Social Security benefits or if your benefits are too small to cover the cost). You will pay for your Part D drug plan premium separately.

PLEASE REMEMBER

☐ It is extremely important that you review the formulary, both before you purchase your Part D drug card and each year after that during open enrollment (October 15 to December 7). With the prices of brand name and injectable medications being as high as they are, not checking the formulary could cost you hundreds or thousands of dollars in uncovered prescriptions.

☐ Even if you don't currently take any prescription medications, we always suggest that you get a Part D drug card (unless you have a Medicare Advantage Plan with drug coverage). There are options that are very inexpensive (usually between $15 and $20 per month) that will keep you from incurring a permanent, increasing, late enrollment penalty. More important, you will have coverage in case you need to get a prescription down the road. We have seen antibiotics and eye drops that cost hundreds of dollars for just one month of therapy. It just makes good sense to get a plan.

CONCLUSION

Choosing an Insurance Agent or Broker

One of our clients, Robert, told us that when he was sixty-four and nine months (in July), he went on vacation to his time-share in Florida. He has done this for quite a few years now, and he's never stopped the delivery of his mail for the one week he's gone. In the past it had never been a concern—but when he got home this year, he stopped his car at his mailbox and found that it was empty. *That's strange*, he thought to himself. *There should have at least been junk mail.*

He drove the rest of the way up his driveway, and now he could see why the mailbox had been empty. On his front steps was an enormous, bundled pile of mail. The stack of envelopes from just one week had obviously been too thick to fit in the mailbox. When Robert got out of the car and started looking through the mail, he discovered that most of it was one form or another of Medicare advertisements. There were large envelopes from insurance companies and smaller letters from local agents and agencies, all wanting to show him the best way to handle his upcoming Medicare decision.

This sounds ridiculous, but it really happened. We have several clients who saved all the Medicare mailings to show us, and the mailings were easily over a foot and a half high when you piled them up. There must be a reason for all of this mail, right?

The reason you get so much mail is that CMS has strict guidelines on how an agent or company can contact you. What all these companies want is for you to contact *them* in some form. The CMS guidelines call this "permission to call" (PTC). Without PTC, it is against regulations for an agent or company to cold call you.

There are exceptions to this rule: for example, it's okay to call prospective customers about Medigap plans. The problem here, however, is this: how does an agent know that you would be best served by a Medigap plan before he or she talks with you? You may be best off with a Medicare Advantage Plan, but if the agent has cold called you, he or she can't sell you one of those. If the agent does, it will be a violation of CMS regulations.

The CMS regulations are there because there have been situations where unscrupulous people have taken advantage of seniors. So, as you approach your sixty-fifth birthday, go through your Medicare mail when it starts arriving. If you see something that is interesting to you, you need to fill out the business reply card, send an e-mail requesting more information, or simply make a phone call. This will allow the agent or company to provide you with the information you're interested in and will keep CMS happy. Remember, a good agent will follow these guidelines. Ones that don't are suspect.

Did you know that the majority of Medigap and Medicare Advantage Plans are purchased over the phone with someone working at a call center or insurance company? It's true, and we view this as a lost opportunity. We don't mean it's a lost opportunity for us—it's a lost opportunity for *you*.

You have the right to work with a local agent or broker: someone who will be there to answer questions and take care of service issues for you—someone who can make this process far easier for you. Don't miss the opportunity to start a relationship that can help you now and in the future. Interview several local agents and find the one you're comfortable with. Ask the following questions:

1. Are the agents licensed and in good standing with your state's Department of Insurance (DOI)? You can check this by going to your state's DOI website and searching for the agents in question. You can also see whom they are appointed with (what companies they represent).

2. Do they represent just one company (captive agents), or are they independent agents? In most cases, you want an independent agent, as they can shop around the marketplace and make sure you have the best plan for your needs.

3. Do they have an office location, or do they work out of their home or car? In most cases, you want agents who are working out of an office; they will have support staff so that you can get a question answered even if the agent is not available at the time of your call. Agents with offices are also more likely to be there in the future.

4. Are they quick to tell you that all the plans are the same and that you should be looking at the least expensive plan? The rate history of the insurance company offering the plan is as important as the actual rate they are charging. Remember, you want the best value for your dollar. Value is not just price; it's also the price you'll pay in the future—five, ten, even fifteen years down the road.

5. Do they represent both Medigap and Medicare Part C Advantage Plans? It's important that they represent both types of plans so they can offer you the plan that works best for your situation. If they only represent one type of plan, then they will find the best plan from what they sell—not what's best for you.

6. Can they provide you with references from their current clients? All agents talk about their "level of service." It's great that they provide a high level of service, but ask them to prove it. Talking with other

clients can give you insight into how agents operate. For example, do they return phone calls in a timely manner? When they tell you they will get you an answer on an issue, do they follow up? In short, do they walk the talk?

Remember, the cost for a Medigap or Medicare Part C Plan is the same regardless of where or how you buy it. Whether you use an agent or a broker or call the insurance company, the cost is the same.

So wouldn't you rather have someone help you build your Medicare blueprint? Wouldn't you like to have someone who can help you understand this important plan for your future? Don't you want someone who will be there after you purchase a plan, in case you have any problems?

And let us repeat one more time. *It won't cost you anything!* It's a win-win situation for both you and the agent/broker.

If we can be of any help to you, even if it's just to answer some questions, please don't hesitate to give us a call. We'd love to help you create the Medicare blueprint that's right for you.

—Jason Mackey & Tim Hanbury

APPENDIX A

Part B Income Related Monthly Adjustment Amount (IRMAA)

The Income Related Monthly Adjustment Amount is based on your modified adjusted gross income (MAGI) from two years ago. If your MAGI is above a certain amount, you will incur a surcharge to your Part B premium.

If your yearly MAGI income in 2015 was:			You pay each month (in 2017)
File individual tax return	**File joint tax return**	**File married and separate tax return**	
$85,000 or less	$170,000 or less	$85,000 or less	$134.00
Above $85,000 up to $107,000	Above $170,000 up to $214,000	Not applicable	$187.50
Above $107,000 up to $160,000	Above $214,000 up to $320,000	Not applicable	$267.90
Above $160,000 up to $214,000	Above $320,000 up to $428,000	Above $85,000 up to $129,000	$348.30
Above $214,000	Above $428,000	Above $129,000	$428.60

APPENDIX B

Plan F: Medicare (Part A) – Hospital Services – Per Benefit Period

A benefit period begins on the first day you receive service as an inpatient in a hospital and ends after you have been out of the hospital and have not received skilled care in any other facility for sixty days in a row.

SERVICES	MEDICARE PAYS	PLAN F PAYS	YOU PAY
HOSPITALIZATION* Semi-private room and board, general nursing, and miscellaneous services and supplies			
First 60 days	All but $1,316	$1,316 (Part A Deductible)	$0
61st thru 90th day	All but $329 per day	$329 per day	$0
91st day and after:			
while using 60 lifetime reserve days	All but $658 per day	$658 per day	$0
once lifetime reserve days are used, additional 365 days	$0	100% of Medicare Eligible Expenses	$0**
beyond the additional 365 days	$0	$0	All costs

SKILLED NURSING FACILITY CARE* You must meet Medicare's requirements, including having been in a hospital for at least 3 days and entering a Medicare-approved facility within 30 days after leaving the hospital			
First 20 days	All approved amounts	$0	$0
21st thru 100th day	All but $164.50 per day	Up to $164.50 per day	$0
101st day and after	$0	$0	All costs
BLOOD			
First 3 pints	$0	3 pints	$0
Additional amounts	100%	$0	$0
HOSPICE CARE			
You must meet Medicare's requirements, including a doctor's certification of terminal illness	All but a very limited copayment/ coinsurance for outpatient drugs and inpatient respite care	Medicare copayment/ coinsurance	$0

**Notice: When your Medicare Part A hospital benefits are exhausted, the insurer stands in the place of Medicare and will pay whatever amount Medicare would have paid for up to an additional 365 days as provided in the policy's "Core Benefits." During this time, the hospital is prohibited from billing you for the balance based on any difference between its billed charges and the amount Medicare would have paid.*

Plan F: Medicare (Part B) – Medical Services – Per Calendar Year

Once you have been billed $183 of the Medicare-approved amounts for covered services (which are noted with an asterisk), your Part B deductible will have been met for the calendar year.

SERVICES	MEDICARE PAYS	PLAN F PAYS	YOU PAY
MEDICAL EXPENSES – IN OR OUR OF THE HOSPITAL AND OUTPATIENT HOSPITAL TREATMENT such as physician's services, inpatient and outpatient medical and surgical services and supplies, physical and speech therapy, diagnostic tests, durable medical equipment			
First $183 of Medicare-approved amounts*	$0	$183 (Part B Deductible)	$0
Remainder of Medicare-approved amounts	Generally 80%	Generally 20%	$0
PART B EXCESS CHARGES			
(above Medicare-approved amounts)	$0	100%	$0
BLOOD			
First 3 pints	$0	All costs	$0
Next $183 of Medicare-approved amounts*	$0	$183 (Part B Deductible)	$0
Remainder of Medicare-approved amounts	80%	20%	$0
CLINICAL LABORATORY SERVICES			
Tests for diagnostic services	100%	$0	$0

Parts A & B

SERVICES	MEDICARE PAYS	PLAN F PAYS	YOU PAY
HOME HEALTH CARE MEDICARE-APPROVED SERVICES			
Medically necessary skilled care services and medical supplies	100%	$0	$0
Durable medical equipment			
First $183 of Medicare-approved amounts*	$0	$183 (Part B Deductible)	$0
Remainder of Medicare-approved amounts	80%	20%	$0

Plan F: Medicare (Part B) – Medical Services – Per Calendar Year (cont'd.)
Other Benefits – Not Covered by Medicare

SERVICES	MEDICARE PAYS	PLAN F PAYS	YOU PAY
FOREIGN TRAVEL – NOT COVERED BY MEDICARE Medically necessary emergency care services beginning during the first 60 days of each trip outside the USA			
First $250 each calendar year	$0	$0	$250
Remainder of charges	$0	80% to a lifetime maximum benefit of $50,000	20% and amounts over $50,000 lifetime maximum

APPENDIX C

Medigap Guaranteed Issue Rights

Guaranteed issue rights are rights you have in certain situations when insurance companies must offer you certain Medigap policies. In these situations, an insurance company:

- must sell you a Medigap policy
- must cover all your preexisting health conditions
- can't charge you more for a Medigap policy because of past or present health problems

1. *You're in a Medicare Advantage Plan, and your plan is leaving Medicare or stops giving care in your area, or you move out of the plan's service area.*

   You have the right to buy Medigap Plan A, B, C, F, K, or L that's sold by any insurance company in your state.

   You only have this right if you switch to Original Medicare rather than joining another Medicare Advantage Plan.

   You can/must apply for a Medigap policy:

- as early as sixty days before the date your coverage will end

- no later than sixty-three calendar days after your coverage ends

Medigap coverage can't start until your Medicare Advantage Plan coverage ends.

2. *You have Original Medicare and an employer group health plan (including retiree or COBRA coverage) or union coverage that pays after Medicare pays, and that plan is ending.*

   You have the right to buy Medigap Plan A, B, C, F, K, or L that's sold by any insurance company in your state.

   If you have COBRA coverage, you can either buy a Medigap policy right away or wait until the COBRA coverage ends.

   You can/must apply for a Medigap policy no later than sixty-three calendar days after the **latest** of these three dates:

   - date the coverage ends

   - date on the notice you get informing you that coverage is ending (if you get one)

   - date on a claim denial, if this is the only way you know that your coverage ended

3. *You joined a Medicare Advantage Plan when you were first eligible for Medicare Part A at sixty-five, and within the first year of joining, you decide you want to switch to Original Medicare (trial right).*

    You have the right to buy any Medigap policy that's sold by any insurance company in your state.

    You can/must apply for a Medigap policy:

    -   as early as sixty calendar days before the date your coverage will end

    -   no later than sixty-three calendar days after your coverage ends

4. *You dropped a Medigap policy to join a Medicare Advantage Plan for the first time, you've been in the plan less than a year, and you want to switch back (trial right).*

    You have the right to buy the Medigap policy you had before you joined the Medicare Advantage Plan if the same insurance company you had before still sells it.

    If your former Medigap policy *isn't* available, you can buy a Medigap Plan A, B, C, F, K, or L that's sold by any insurance company in your state.

    You can/must apply for a Medigap policy:

    -   as early as sixty calendar days before the date your coverage will end

- no later than sixty-three calendar days after your coverage ends

5. *Your Medigap insurance company goes bankrupt and you lose your coverage, or your Medigap policy coverage otherwise ends through no fault of your own.*

   You have the right to buy Medigap Plan A, B, C, F, K, or L that's sold by any insurance company in your state.

   You can/must apply for a Medigap policy no later than sixty-three calendar days from the date your coverage ends.

6. *You leave a Medicare Advantage Plan or drop a Medigap policy because the company hasn't followed the rules, or it misled you.*

   You have the right to buy Medigap Plan A, B, C, F, K, or L that's sold by any insurance company in your state.

   You can/must apply for a Medigap policy no later than sixty-three calendar days from the date your coverage ends.

APPENDIX D

Example of Health Questions Asked by Insurance Companies If You Are Outside of Your IEP, SEP, or a Guarantee Issue Right

1. In the last five years, have you had medical or surgical advice, treatment, or consultation for any of the following conditions?			
a.	Yes	No	Heart attack, congestive heart failure, heart failure, enlarged heart, or heart procedure or surgery (prior or not yet performed); aneurysm; peripheral vascular disease (poor circulation in your extremities); any stent placement; stroke or transient ischemic attack (TIA)?
b.	Yes	No	Emphysema, chronic obstructive pulmonary disease (COPD), chronic bronchitis, tuberculosis, or other chronic lung disorder (excluding mild or moderate asthma)?
c.	Yes	No	Chronic kidney disease, kidney failure, or kidney dialysis?
d.	Yes	No	Crippling or disabling arthritis or bone disease, osteoporosis with fracture(s), or hip replacement?
e.	Yes	No	Alzheimer's disease, dementia, organic brain disorder, any senility disorder, Parkinson's disease, multiple sclerosis, amyotrophic lateral sclerosis (ALS), or systemic lupus?
f.	Yes	No	Internal cancer, malignant melanoma, leukemia, Hodgkin's disease, lymphoma, or bone marrow or organ transplant (except cornea)?
g.	Yes	No	Diabetes in addition to any of the following: diabetic retinopathy, peripheral vascular disease, neuropathy, any heart condition (including high blood pressure), *ever* had any amputation due to diabetes, or *ever* required more than fifty units of insulin daily?
h.	Yes	No	Alcohol or drug abuse or misuse, cirrhosis of the liver, or other chronic liver disease?
i.	Yes	No	Acquired immune deficiency syndrome (AIDS), AIDS-related complex (ARC), or the human immunodeficiency virus (HIV)

j.	Yes	No	Are you currently totally disabled, bedridden, hospitalized, or confined to a nursing or other facility?
2.	Yes	No	Do you need assistance, supervision, or a wheelchair for any daily activities such as dressing, eating, bathing, or walking?
3.		In the last two years:	
a.	Yes	No	Have you had medical advice, treatment, or consultation for any psychological, psychiatric, mental, or nervous disorders?
b.	Yes	No	Have you been advised or recommended to receive treatment for any condition that would require surgery, hospitalization, or confinement to a facility?
c.	Yes	No	Have you been advised by a physician to have medical tests, treatment, or therapy that has not been performed?
d.	Yes	No	Have you taken or been prescribed three or more prescription medications on a regular basis?

If you answer "yes" to the above questions, please provide details below:

4.	Yes	No	Have you used tobacco in any form in the last two years?
5.	Yes	No	Are you a diabetic controlled by diet or oral medications?
6.	Yes	No	In the last twelve months, have you taken or been prescribed any prescription medications? If "yes", please provide details for all medication below.

Medication	Date Start/Stopped	Dosage/Frequency	Reason for Medication

APPENDIX E

Typical Summary of Benefits for a Part C Medicare Advantage Plan

Medical Benefits	In-Network	Out-of-Network
Annual out-of-pocket maximum*	$6,700 in-network	$6,700 combined in and out-of-network
Doctor's office visit	Primary care provider: $30 copay Specialist: $50 copay (no referral needed)	Primary care provider: $30 copay Specialist: $50 copay (no referral needed)
Preventive services	$0 copay	$0 copay
Inpatient hospital care	$395 copay per day: days 1–4 $0 copay per day after that	$395 copay per day: days 1–4 $0 copay per day after that
Skilled nursing facility (SNF)	$0 copay per day: days 1–20 $160 copay per day: days 21–62 $0 copay per day: days 63–100	$0 copay per day: days 1–20 $160 copay per day: days 21–62 $0 copay per day: days 63–100
Outpatient surgery	20% of the cost	20% of the cost
Diabetes monitoring supplies	$0 copay for covered brands	20% of the cost
Home health care	$0 copay	50% of the cost
Diagnostic tests and procedures (such as MRIs, CT scans)	20% of the cost	20% of the cost

Diagnostic tests and procedures (non-radiological)	20% of the cost	20% of the cost
Lab services	$16 copay	$16 copay
Outpatient x-rays	$16 copay	$16 copay
Ambulance	$250 copay	$250 copay
Emergency care	$75 copay (worldwide)	
Urgently needed services	$30–$40 copay ($75 copay for worldwide coverage)	

*The most you may pay in a year for medical care

Benefits and Services beyond Original Medicare		
	In-Network	**Out-of-Network**
Routine physical	$0 copay; 1 per year*	$0 copay; 1 per year*
Vision—routine eye exams	$25 copay; 1 every year	$25 copay; 1 every year
Vision—eyewear	$0 copay every year; up to $100 for lenses/frames and contacts*	$0 copay every year; up to $100 for lenses/frames and contacts*
Dental	$20 copay for office visit (includes exam, cleaning, x-rays, denture adjustments)*	$20 copay for office visit (includes exam, cleaning, x-rays, denture adjustments)*
Foot care—routine exam	$50 copay; 6 visits per year*	$50 copay; 6 visits per year*
Hearing—routine exam	$20 copay; 1 per year*	$20 copay; 1 per year*
Hearing aids	$390–$450 copay for each hearing aid*	$390–$450 copay for each hearing aid*
Nurse on call	Speak with a registered nurse (RN) 24 hours a day, 7 days a week	

*Benefits combined in and out-of-network

Prescription Drugs		
	Your Cost	
Annual prescription deductible	$0 for Tier 1 and Tier 2; $205 for Tier 3, Tier 4, and Tier 5	
Initial coverage stage	**Standard Retail**	**Preferred Mail Order**
	(30-day)	(90-day)
Tier 1: Preferred generic drugs	$2 copay	$0 copay
Tier 2: Generic drugs	$12 copay	$0 copay
Tier 3: Preferred brand drugs	$47 copay	$131 copay
Tier 4: Non-preferred brand drugs	$100 copay	$290 copay
Tier 5: Specialty tier drugs	28% of the cost	28% of the cost
Coverage gap stage	After your total drug costs reach $3,700, you will pay no more than 51% of the total cost for generic drugs or 40% of the total cost for brand-name drugs, for any drug tier during the coverage gap.	
Catastrophic coverage stage	After your total out-of-pocket costs reach $4,950, you will pay the greater of $3.30 copay for generic (including brand drugs treated as generic), $8.25 copay for all other drugs, or 5% of the cost.